FOURTH EDITION

SENTENCE-COMBINING WORKBOOK

FOURTH EDITION

SENTENCE-COMBINING WORKBOOK

Pam Altman
San Francisco State University

Mari Caro
San Francisco State University

Lisa Metge-Egan

Leslie Roberts

Australia • Brazil • Japan • Korea • Mexico • Singapore • Spain • United Kingdom • United States

WADSWORTH
CENGAGE Learning

Sentence-Combining Workbook, Fourth Edition
Pam Altman, Mari Caro, Lisa Metge-Egan, Leslie Roberts

Director of Developmental Studies: Annie Todd

Assistant Editor: Elizabeth Rice

Editorial Assistant: Luria Rittenberg

Media Editor: Christian Biagetti

Brand Manager: Lydia LeStar

Sr. MarComm Manager: Linda Yip

Rights Acquisitions Specialist: Ann Hoffman

Manufacturing Planner: Betsy Donaghey

Art and Design Direction, Production Management, and Composition: PreMediaGlobal

Cover Image: ©luchunyu/Shutterstock

Library of Congress Control Number: 2012954711

ISBN-13: 978-1-285-17711-3

ISBN-10: 1-285-17711-8

Wadsworth
20 Channel Center Street
Boston, MA 02210
USA

Cengage Learning is a leading provider of customized learning solutions with office locations around the globe, including Singapore, the United Kingdom, Australia, Mexico, Brazil and Japan. Locate your local office at **international.cengage.com/region**

Cengage Learning products are represented in Canada by Nelson Education, Ltd.

For your course and learning solutions, visit **www.cengage.com.**

Purchase any of our products at your local college store or at our preferred online store **www.cengagebrain.com.**

Instructors: Please visit **login.cengage.com** and log in to access instructor-specific resources.

Printed in the United States of America
1 2 3 4 5 6 7 16 15 14 13 12

Contents

Preface

To the Student

Most writers, whether experienced or inexperienced, sometimes feel that they just can't get their good ideas down on paper, that something gets lost when they try to express themselves in written words. This book aims to help you become more aware of, and be able to use, a variety of ways to express your ideas in the writing that you do for college courses, in your personal lives, and in your future careers.

Throughout this book, you will practice using a variety of sentence-combining and sentence-expanding techniques so that you will be able to communicate your ideas in fluent, concise, and clear sentence structures. You will find that each unit in this book focuses on a specific sentence-level technique and that most of the sentence-combining exercises within the units tell a story. To make the best use of this book, you should write out all of the solutions to the exercises, read them aloud to make sure your solutions sound right, and finally, proofread them to make sure that you haven't made any errors. And most important, you should use the techniques you practice in the exercises when you write the essays you are working on in your writing course.

If you devote your time and energy to the work of this book, paying close attention with your classmates to the way language works, letting your teacher know whenever you have questions, and applying what you learn to your essay writing, you'll see great improvement in your writing and find that you really can get your good ideas down on paper.

To the Teacher

This book represents a commitment to sentence combining as the most efficient and productive approach to sentence-level skill-building in the basic writing classroom. Units in this book have also been used at levels other than basic writing—in English as a Second Language composition, freshman composition, and remedial writing classes for students of all ages, including international graduate students.

Some studies have also found that basic writers particularly gain from sentence combining—a positive approach that emphasizes the enjoyment of skill-building rather than error avoidance and that builds students' confidence as they see real results in their writing.

But sentence combining cannot be an end in itself; we see the work of this book as the skills-building component of a college composition course in which students analyze information and ideas, making inferences and establishing logical relationships for a purpose.

This book has been used in the basic writing classes at San Francisco State University (SFSU) for several years. Originally written in 1989 and distributed for use at SFSU, it has since undergone many revisions at the suggestions of the editors at Cengage Learning, SFSU composition instructors, Bay Area community college instructors, reviewers from across the country and students in the basic writing classes themselves, both native speakers of English and bilingual students. The principal author taught a minimum of four basic writing courses per year for 15 years.

New to the Fourth Edition

To enhance our student writers' engagement and success with sentence-level techniques that help them achieve fluency, variety, and even confidence in their writing, we have made several changes in the fourth edition.

The key update to this edition is the new Unit 2: Recognizing Clauses. In response to market feedback, we have added this chapter with the goal of helping students recognize independent and dependent clauses, as well as how to punctuate when using clauses in writing. Throughout this text, we have added revised and updated exercises and clarified instructions. Among the new exercises are those that provide more opportunities for students to create their own sentences after they have practiced a technique, making connections between the writing they do in this workbook and their "real" writing. In addition to these open exercises, we have created new exercises whose subject matter should appeal to a range of students, from young college-age students to older students returning to school or attending college for the first time.

A valuable addition to this book is an Answer Key, provided so that instructors can devote more energy to teaching than to correcting students' work. The Answer Key is posted on the Instructor Companion Site for Altman, *Sentence-Combining Workbook*, 4e. Also available on the Instructor Companion Site are the Final Review Exercises in formats that allow for editing and downloading for classroom use. Instructors can access these resources through login.cengage.com.

How to Use This Book

This book is divided into two main sections: sentence joining and sentence modifying, both of which are organized to provide students with practice combining sets of sentences to produce more specific, concise, and fluent sentences. Throughout this book, the emphasis is on doing, rather than analyzing the grammatical structures under practice. Thus, we have avoided extensive explanations about parts of speech or rhetorical purpose.

If you do not feel that your particular class needs a unit, you should adjust the book to fit the needs of your class by skipping a unit or modifying it. But you should consider carefully the review units, which make use of previously practiced techniques.

We recommend that students spend two 30-minute sessions each week on sentence combining. Most units have the same format: an introduction to the technique to be practiced, an exercise to be done in class, and a follow-up homework exercise. We suggest that the instructor introduce the technique before turning to the book. We also suggest doing the first exercise collaboratively—having students recite their answers to the first two or three sentence sets and then work in pairs on the remaining sets. One student in each pair should write their answer on the board, and once all students have finished and the entire exercise is on the board, the authors should read their answers aloud as the class focuses on each one. This class work gives the instructor the chance to praise success, offer help, and reiterate the essential messages about form and meaning, and it promotes students' attentiveness to language use. Board work also sometimes turns up usage problems, which should always be addressed after the sentence combining has been evaluated. Students should be encouraged to ask questions or to suggest alternatives. To deal with homework exercises, the instructor can ask students to compare their homework with another student's to see if they disagree. Exercises should be collected and graded. The students should write out all of their answers if the exercises are to have any effect on their writing, and most important, the instructor should always relate the technique under practice to the students' current writing assignment.

Units One and Two are introductory units; Unit One reviews the basic sentence, giving as little in the way of grammar terminology as possible, and serves as background to Unit Two. Unit Two introduces sentence focus, which is both an approach to expressing complex ideas and an editing technique. Composition instructors are of mixed opinions about teaching focus at the basic writing level; some believe that it should be reserved for higher-level courses, while others believe that basic writers will overcome sentence focus problems just with writing practice and helpful feedback. We know that some basic writers, inexperienced with academic discourse, attempt what they believe to be academic writing by overusing abstract sentence subjects and passive verbs, an approach that for some writers is just a developmental stage. But we believe that teaching sentence focus is helpful for basic writers, some of whom produce sentences that are so poorly constructed that the writers themselves don't know why they wrote them—or what they meant to say. Anyone who has taught basic writing must have been at one time or another dismayed by seemingly unclassifiable problems at the sentence level (customarily labeled in the essay margins as "awkward" or "predication error," labels that do nothing to help the basic writer). We believe that teaching sentence focus is a reliable way to approach these problems without burdening students with useless grammar lessons or vague error correction. With genuine writing practice and sentence-combining practice, most students will overcome these problems, but the sentence focus guidelines give them a nudge. However, if you are uncommitted to the sentence focus approach, you can skip to Unit Four.

The Review Sections throughout the book are cued exercises (exercises that signal the technique to be used) and should be self-explanatory. The Review Section at the end of the book contains exercises that are not cued but have been carefully written and assessed to allow students to create sentences using the techniques they have practiced in the book.

Semester after semester, in their course evaluations, students write that sentence combining helped them grow as writers and that they had fun doing it. That's what we hope for—that sentence combining will be both enjoyable and purposeful for both students and instructors.

Acknowledgments

We want to express our gratitude to the reviewers of this book for their careful evaluation of the text and for their many thoughtful suggestions.

Reviewers of the Fourth Edition

Lyttron Burris, Grand Rapids Community College
Tristan Saldana, Contra Costa College
Dan Clark, Moreno Valley College
Tammy White, Forsyth Technical College
Barbara Davis, Yavapai College
Ken Kerr, Frederick Community College
Jim Wilkins-Luton, Clark College
Virginia Smith, Carteret Community College
Jenny Cogswell, Hartnell College

Reviewers of the Third Edition

Jeff Mitchell, Los Medanos College
Andrea Schriner, San Francisco State University
Kelly Vogel, City College of San Francisco
Sarah Watson, East Texas Baptist University
Karen Wong, Skyline College

Reviewers of the Second Edition

Patricia Johnson, Broward Community College
Deirdre Rowley, Imperial Valley College
Brian Strang, San Francisco State University
Karen Wong, Skyline College

Reviewers of the First Edition

Michael Guista, Allan Hancock College
Jeffrey Mitchell, Los Medanos College
Susan Reiger, Porterville College
Karen Wong, Skyline College
Susan Zimmerman, City College of San Francisco

Unit One

The Basic Sentence

Throughout this book, you will be combining sentences to practice ways to show logical relationships or to modify, or describe, words in sentences. This practice will help you express your ideas in clear, concise, and varied sentences when you write college-level essays. But first it helps to know what makes a sentence a sentence. Look at the following groups of words; which do you think are complete sentences?

(a) Teenagers work.
(b) Many teenagers work after school.
(c) Many teenagers work after school to earn spending money.

If you think that all three are sentences, you are correct, because all three contain a subject-verb unit—a subject and verb working together. Sentence (a) has a verb, the word *work*; it's a verb because it can change form to show the time or tense of an action. So we can say:

Teenagers worked.
Teenagers will work.

Sentence (a) also has a subject, *teenagers*, a word that does the action in the verb. Because sentence (a) has a subject-verb unit, *teenagers work*, it is a complete sentence. Sentences (b) and (c) are also complete sentences; they have the same subject-verb unit as sentence (a) in addition to sentence modifiers that tell more about the subject and verb.

Take a look at the following groups of words; which do you think are complete sentences?

(a) They are.
(b) They are students.
(c) They are students hoping to succeed in college.

Again, all three are complete sentences because they each contain a subject-verb unit—*they are*. But in these sentences, the verb doesn't name an action; the verb is a form of *be*. The common forms of *be* are *am*, *is*, *are*, *was*, *were*, *has been*, *have been*, and *will be*.

To write well, you don't need to know how to identify all of the parts of speech. But if you know how verbs and subjects work together in sentences, you'll find the upcoming work in this book easier, which in turn should help you grow as a writer as you work on focusing, joining, and developing your sentences. In some of the later units, you'll see references to "subjects," "verbs," and "verb forms," so you will benefit in a practical way from the overview of subjects and verbs in this unit.

Recognizing Verbs

You probably know the common definition of verbs—*words that show action or existence*—but that definition is not always helpful when you need to find the subject-verb unit that makes a group of words a sentence. The most reliable way to identify subject-verb units in sentences is to find the verb first and then the subject. To locate the verbs in sentences, you must find the action words or forms of *be* that you can change the tense (time) of.

Exercise One On Tour with the Band

From each pair of sentences below, you can create one sentence by joining the verbs (with *and* or *or*) and eliminating repeated words.

EXAMPLE: The rock band travels around the United States. The rock band plays concerts.

SOLUTION: The rock band travels around the United States and plays concerts.

1. The lead singer sings.
   The lead singer talks to the audience.

2. Some of the people cheer.
   Some of the people clap.

3. Others in the crowd stage dive.
   Others dance in the audience.

4. The security staff watches.
   The security staff worries about the crowd.

5. The band finishes their concert.
   The band runs to their tour bus.

Exercise Two The Last Band Tour

Now go back to the sentences in Exercise One and rewrite your combined sentences to show that the actions happened in a *past* band tour. (You can begin the sentences with *last year*.) Then underline the words you changed to show past time, or tense.

EXAMPLE: The rock band travels around the United States. The rock band plays concerts.

SOLUTION: (Last year) The rock band traveled around the United States and played concerts.

1.

2.

3.

4.

5.

The words you changed and underlined are verbs—words that show the time, or tense, of an action, or a form of *be*, in a sentence.

Finding verbs can sometimes be difficult because we often use verb forms as other parts of speech. For example, one form of the word *swim* can be used as a verb, but with an *-ing* ending, it can also be used as a noun (a word naming a person, place, or thing) or an adjective (a word describing a noun).

Alicia swims a mile every lunch hour.	(*swims* = verb)
Swimming is Alicia's favorite way to relax.	(*swimming* = noun)
Alicia would like nothing better than to have her own swimming pool.	(*swimming* = adjective describing *pool*)

The noun *swimming* and the adjective *swimming* do not change to show the time, or tense, of the sentence. If Alicia decided to give up swimming and start meditating for relaxation, we might write:

Swimming was Alicia's favorite way to relax.

The verb *is* changes to *was* to show past time, but the word *swimming* doesn't change because it isn't acting as a verb here. An *-ing* word can only be part of a verb if it follows a form of the verb *be*:

In her dreams, Alicia <u>is swimming</u> in her own pool.

Exercise Three Sing Me to Sleep

In each sentence, change each main verb to past time, or tense. Underline the verb; then put in parentheses any verb forms that *don't* change to show time.

EXAMPLE: Listening to music relaxes me.

SOLUTION: (Listening) to music relaxed me last night.

1. I listen to music on the radio.

2. The DJ bores me by reading so many details about the singers.

3. His boring voice puts me to sleep.

4. I follow the new releases of my favorite musicians.

5. Johnny Cash writes songs that I like.

6. I often dream of writing a hit song.

7. But for someone like Johnny Cash writing a hit song takes talent and luck.

Using a Dictionary to Choose the Correct Verb Form

To change verb tense, we change the form of the verb, which simply means that we add something on the end of the base form (*walk* becomes *walked* to show past tense) or change its spelling (*bring* becomes *brought* to show past tense).

You can find the correct forms of verbs in a dictionary. Look up the base form. Often you know the base form (the form you use with *to*—*to walk, to sing, to swim*).

If you don't know the base form of the verb, you can find it by looking up any form other than the base form. For instance, if you look up the word *sank* in the dictionary, it will direct you to the *to* form of the verb—*sink*.

Once you find the base form, dictionaries list the other verb forms in the same order:

1. **base form**	2. **past**	3. **past participle** (follows *has* or *have*)	4. **present participle** (follows a *be* form)
walk	walked	walked	walking
create	created	created	creating

Like many languages, English has regular and irregular verbs. Regular verbs such as *walk* and *create* all show the tense, or time, the same way; for instance, we add an *-ed* or a *-d* to the end of regular verbs to indicate past tense. If a verb is regular, the past and past participle forms are the same, so the dictionary will only list the base and the past forms. To make the past participle forms (forms after *have* or *had*) or the present participle forms (*-ing* forms), you just add the *-ed* or *-ing* ending to the base form.

Verbs that don't follow this predictable pattern are called irregular verbs.

1. **base form**	2. **past**	3. **past participle**	4. **present participle**
be	was/were	been	being
eat	ate	eaten	eating
meet	met	met	meeting

Many of our verbs are irregular, and you may not know all of the past and past participle forms. Sometimes the past and past participle forms of irregular verbs are the same, but sometimes they are not. Any time you aren't sure what a verb's past or past participle form is, you must look it up in a dictionary.

Exercise Four Write/Wrote/Written

To review some commonly confused irregular verbs, use a dictionary to find the past tense and the past participle forms of the base form verbs listed below.

Base	Past Tense	Past Participle
1. become		
2. begin		
3. broke		
4. choose		
5. come		
6. do		
7. get		
8. give		
9. go		
10. prove		
11. put		
12. ride		
13. rise		
14. run		
15. see		

Exercise Five Getting a Record

In the following sentences, you are given the past tense of verbs. Change each sentence from past tense to past perfect (with *have* or *has*) by putting the correct past participle in each blank space.

1. Mark and his friends drove to the record store.

   Mark and his friends have ______________ to the record store many times.

2. They got into an accident on the freeway.

   They have ______________ into accidents on the freeway before.

3. The police led them to the station to file a report.

   The police have ______________ many drivers there.

4. Now Mark has a bad driving record.

   Mark has ______________ a bad driving record since he was 16.

Exercise Six The Onion Cure

Write the correct past tense or past participle verb form for the verbs given in their base forms. Those in parentheses should be put in past tense form; those in brackets should be put in the past participle form after *have* or *has*.

Not many people ______________ [hear] of an unpopular but infallible cold remedy that my friend Fred recently ______________ (tell) me about. Fred ______________ (eat) a large raw onion and ______________ (swear) that it ______________ (be) the best cold remedy ______________ (know). He ______________ (bite) into it like an apple, and though it ______________ (make) his eyes water, he ______________ (think) the potency of the onion ______________ (kill) all the germs in his body. Many times I ______________ [want] to try this magic onion cure, but I ______________ [be] afraid to take the first bite.

Recognizing Subjects

Once you have located the verbs in sentences, it's easier to find the subjects—the words that tell who or what does the action or the form of *be* in the verbs.

To locate verbs and subjects, follow this two-step process:

1. Use the time test to find the verb; change the sentence to another time.

   Alicia swims a mile every lunch hour.
   (last year) Alicia swam a mile every lunch hour.

   To show the change in time, or tense, we changed *swims* to *swam*, so *swims* is the verb.

2. Once you have found the verb, you can locate the subject of the verb by asking yourself:

   Who or what ________*?*
   verb

   Who or what swims a mile every lunch hour?
   verb

   The answer is *Alicia*, so *Alicia* is the subject of the verb swims.

Our example sentence has one subject-verb unit—*Alicia swims*. Often, though, verbs can have more than one subject:

Alicia and Tieu swim a mile every lunch hour.

Or subjects can have more than one verb:

Alicia swims a mile and lifts weights every lunch hour.

Or sentences can have more than one subject-verb unit:

Alicia swims a mile every lunch hour, but then her boss treats her to a cheesesteak for lunch.

Be sure to look at the whole sentence when you follow the two-step process for finding verbs and subjects so that you are sure to locate all of the subject-verb units.

Exercise Seven Mind Your Manners

The following groups of words are not complete sentences because they don't have subjects—words that work together with verbs. In the blanks provided, supply a subject to complete each sentence. (It helps to skim the whole story first.)

EXAMPLE: _______________ have terrible manners.

SOLUTION: Many people have terrible manners.

1. On the freeway,________________________ make you tense by tailgating or blasting their horns.
2. In department stores,________________________ follow you around, suspecting you of shoplifting.
3. ______________________ crowd behind you in line for the ATM, trying to see your bank balance.
4. On the bus,________________________ won't give up their seats for elderly people or students carrying heavy backpacks.
5. In a concert hall,________________________ wear intense cologne spiked with gardenias, vanilla, and cloves.
6. And sometimes in a theater,________________________ loudly analyze the plot all through the movie.
7. In restaurants,________________________ throw tantrums over fifteen-minute waits for their checks.
8. At baseball games,________________________ jump up in front of you right in the middle of a double play.
9. Of all these rude people,________________________ bug me the most.
10. __________________ should take a course on etiquette.

Exercise Eight Get a Job

In this exercise, follow the two steps for identifying verbs and their subjects. Underline the verbs once and the subjects twice. Reminder: An *-ing* word can only be part of a verb if it follows a form of the verb *be*, e.g., *am working* and *was thinking*.

EXAMPLE: Most people work in conventional occupations, such as accounting, teaching, or retail sales.

SOLUTION:

Step 1: To find the verb, change the time, or tense, of the sentence. To change the time, we have to change *work* to *worked*, so *work* is the verb.

Step 2: To find the subject, ask yourself "Who or what works?" The answer is *people*, so *people* is the subject. verb

(*5 years ago*) Most people worked in conventional occupations, such as accounting, teaching, or retail sales.

1. Some people have more interesting careers.
2. They become Guillotine Operators, White-Kid Buffers, or Liquid Runners.
3. A Guillotine Operator cuts pencils, not necks.
4. A White-Kid Buffer operates a leather buffer machine, not white kids.
5. A Liquid Runner in a candy factory regulates the flow of syrup.
6. Some people become Gizzard-Skin Removers in a poultry plant.
7. A close friend working as a Bosom Presser irons blouses in a laundry.
8. Her husband, a Top Screw, is the boss of a bunch of cowpunchers.
9. Working in one of these occupations teaches young people about life in the real world.
10. But after reading about these jobs, most people want to get a college degree.

Exercise Nine Get Up and Move!

In this exercise, follow the two steps for identifying verbs and their subjects. Underline the verbs once and the subjects twice. Reminder: An *-ing* word can only be part of a verb if it follows a form of the verb *be*, e.g., *is eating* and *has been waiting*.

EXAMPLE: Some people exercise for better health.

SOLUTION:

Step 1: To find the verb, change the time, or tense, of the sentence.

(*10 years ago*) Some people exercised for better health.

To change the time, we change *exercise* to *exercised*, so *exercise* is the verb.

Step 2: To find the subject, ask yourself, "Who or what exercises?" The answer is *people*, so *people* is the subject. verb

ANSWER: Some people exercise for better health.

1. Some people run three miles or more a day to stay healthy.
2. Four high-impact hours of aerobic activity a week reduces blood pressure.
3. High-impact activities raise your heart rate.
4. A healthy heart rate can lower your blood pressure.
5. But too much aerobic activity can hurt your joints.
6. People also use low-impact activities like walking to stay fit.
7. Some people worry that walking will not keep them fit.
8. But walking is good for your heart.
9. Swimming is also a good low-impact activity.
10. Swimming reduces the risk of joint or muscle injury.

Unit Two

Recognizing Clauses

A clause is a group of words with both a subject and a verb. There are two kinds of clauses: *independent* clauses or main clauses and dependent clauses or subordinate clauses.

Independent Clauses

Let's start with independent clauses. An independent clause, as its name suggests, can stand on its own in a sentence and sentences can be made up of one or more independent clauses. One independent clause can be joined by another independent clause with a coordinating conjunction like *and*, *but*, or *so*. Using a coordinating conjunction is one way to connect two independent clauses or thoughts.

Here's an example showing that two sentences, when joined by the coordinating conjunction *but*, become one sentence with two individual, but connected, thoughts.

EXAMPLE: Jane didn't want to go to the movies. [but] She went anyway.

SOLUTION: Jane didn't want to go to the movies, but she went anyway.

Other coordinating conjunctions you might see that indicate an independent clause are *yet*, *nor*, *or*, and *for*. If you remember these coordinating conjunctions, you will be able to identify independent clauses without a problem. Here's a quick way to remember your coordinating conjunctions:

FANBOYS

F—For
A—And
N—Nor
B—But
O—Or
Y—Yet
S—So

Exercise One Election Day

In the following sentences, underline the independent clauses.

1. Marnie is involved in local politics, so she works the election booth on voting day.
2. She is responsible for signing in voters, and they like seeing her year after year.
3. Many people arrive early to vote, but they are often in a hurry to get to work.
4. Marnie makes sure that they get in and out, so they can get to work on time.
5. There were many voters at one point, but everyone in line was very polite.
6. Marnie didn't need any help, nor did she ask for it.
7. She likes to greet every voter individually, and they appreciate her personal attention to them.
8. The voters in the town are committed to local politics, for they know how important it is to have the right leadership.
9. Some voters are upset with the results, yet the majority always wins.
10. Marnie thinks local politics is fascinating, and she plans to keep volunteering on election day for years to come.

Exercise Two The Dinner Party

Combine the following independent clauses with a conjunction to make one complete sentence.

1. Anna wanted to have a dinner party on Saturday night.
   She created a guest list.

2. She wanted to invite twelve of her closest friends.
   She didn't have enough chairs to seat everyone.

3. On Thursday, she went to the local party rental company.
   She rented six additional chairs.

4. She had hoped to rent eight.
   The company had only six available for that night.

5. Later, she went to the grocery store.
   She bought some food that she could prepare before the party.

6. Anna thought she remembered the recipe for pasta salad.
   She had forgotten it.

7. She looked up the recipe on her phone.
   She could make it taste delicious.

8. She started boiling water at home.
   She began to make pasta.

9. She downloaded other recipes while she was cooking.
   She could impress her friends with the meal.

10. The night of the party, Anna served dinner.
    Her friends were surprised by what a good cook she was!

Exercise Three A Trip to the Beach

In the following exercise, look at the first sentence and using what you know about coordinating conjunctions and independent clauses, finish the sentence by adding another independent clause in your own words.

1. Jose and Toni decided that they needed a vacation, but ______________________.
2. They decided to take a trip to the beach, and ______________________.
3. When they got there, the sun was hot, but ______________________.
4. The spots closest to the water were all taken by other beachgoers, so ______________.
5. The surf seemed rough, yet ______________________.
6. Jose and Toni relaxed away from the surf, and ______________________.
7. Jose was reading a novel, and ______________________.
8. Toni brought a bagged lunch, but ______________________.
9. Jose bought his lunch at the snack bar, and ______________________.
10. When the day was over, they packed the car, and ______________________.

Dependent Clauses

Dependent clauses are clauses that cannot stand on their own, hence the name *dependent*. In order to make sense and be a grammatically correct part of a sentence, they must be joined to an independent clause. Although dependent clauses contain a subject and a verb, they are still dependent. There are a few different types of dependent clauses; for now, we'll focus on adverb clauses and adjective clauses.

Adverb clauses describe a verb and usually answer the questions "where," "why," "how," or "when." Look for subordinating conjunctions—which you will learn more about in Unit Five—like *after*, *although*, *because*, *if*, *when*, or *until*, to name a few—to indicate that you are looking at a dependent adverbial clause.

Look at the example below to see how two ideas can be joined by a subordinating conjunction so that the sentence makes sense.

Marta will love you forever. Because you bring her flowers.

These two ideas can be joined by *because* to make one fluid and correct sentence:

Marta will love you forever because you bring her flowers.

The dependent clause *because you bring her flowers answers the question why will Marta love you forever?*

An adjective clause describes a noun so when looking for an adjective clause, look for the part of the sentence that starts with a pronoun such as *who*, *which*, or *that*. Sometimes, adjective clauses will start with *when* or *where*. An adjective clause modifies the noun or pronoun that comes before it. Look at the following example.

The cat that I adopted is adorable.

The cat is the subject while *that I adopted* is an adjective clause that modifies the subject of the sentence.

Exercise Four Working on Our Fixer-Upper

In the following sentences, identify whether the underlined clause is an adverb clause or an adjective clause by writing ADV or ADJ below the clause.

1. The house <u>that we bought</u> was in need of repair.

2. The first thing we need to do <u>after we move in</u> is paint the porch.

3. The rest of the painting can wait <u>until we have more time</u>.

4. The neighbor <u>who lives next door</u> is happy we moved in.

5. She likes us <u>because we are committed to fixing up the house</u>.

6. We didn't know where to start <u>when we moved in</u>.

7. So we took a look around <u>until we figured out that painting was first</u>.

8. Although we are very happy there, we have a lot to do.

9. That painting that needs to be done will happen in the cooler weather.

10. Until the weather turns cooler, we will be happy with the way things are.

Exercise Five A Woman's Right to Vote

In the following paragraph, identify whether the underlined clause is an adverb clause or an adjective clause by writing ADV or ADJ below the clause. Then, circle the noun that the clause is modifying.

In 1918, the House of Representatives voted to approve the Nineteenth Amendment because of pressure from the president. The amendment, which would give women the right to vote, was only approved by the Senate, voting fifty-six to twenty-five. Suffragists, which was the name given to women who supported the amendment, kept fighting because they wanted more states to give women the right to vote. Anti-suffragists, the people who didn't think women should vote, kept up their fight as well. Although anti- suffragists made a strong argument for keeping things as they were, suffragists were successful in getting Illinois, Wisconsin, and Michigan as the first states to ratify the law. These states were a benefit to the cause until the suffragists could get more support.

Unit Three

Sentence Focus

At times we read something that doesn't make sense to us, or we write something ourselves, thinking, "That's not what I meant to say" or "This doesn't sound right." Chances are that the writing isn't clearly focused on the subject or topic. Your readers will more easily understand your ideas if you focus them clearly, and it's really not so hard to do. Often clear focus in writing depends on clearly focused sentence subjects.

Read the following paragraph aloud:

> Professor Seed suffered through a disastrous first day as a college professor. (a) The way in which he set his alarm clock was incorrect (b) so the early bus was missed and campus wasn't reached until 30 minutes after his first class began. (c) Then the classroom was appeared at by him. (d) Help was given by many students, (e) but still the wrong classroom was appeared at by him. (f) Finally the realization came that his wallet was lost, (g) so bus fare had to be borrowed. (h) At home that night, he was told by his wife that the reason he had a bad day was because the wrong foot was started off on.

This paragraph begins with a topic sentence, a sentence that tells the main idea of the paragraph. The topic sentence makes it clear that the subject of the paragraph will be Professor Seed, specifically his first day as a college professor. Yet the focus of the rest of the paragraph isn't clear because Professor Seed, the subject of the paragraph and the grammatical subject of the first sentence, never again appears as a sentence subject.

This paragraph, then, is unfocused; it's hard to figure out who did what. By focusing your sentences clearly, you can make sure that your reader understands who performs the action or form of *be* in the verb.

You can do a few things to make your writing more interesting to the reader. You can vary sentence length—using both short and long sentences—think about your word choices, and use the correct tense in your writing. Another is to use "active voice" in your writing, writing in a way so that the subject is doing the action. Here's an example of active versus passive voice:

Active: Jenna walked the dog.
Passive: The dog is being walked by Jenna.

Do you see the difference? In the first sentence, Jenna, the subject, is doing the action. In the second, the dog, who is doing nothing but being walked, is the subject. Making sure your subjects are doing the action is one key to writing an interesting paragraph or essay.

In this unit, you will work on applying guidelines for writing focused sentences, which in turn will help you keep larger pieces of writing focused.

Here are the two basic guidelines:

- When you begin to write, ask yourself, "What subject am I writing about?" The subject/topic of your writing will often be the sentence subject.
- Ask yourself, "Who (or what) does what?" The answer should be the sentence subject.

Exercise One Hard Ball

Each of the following sentences begins well, but the parts in parentheses aren't focused clearly. In the blanks provided, rewrite the parts in parentheses so that you keep the focus on the personal, human subject. Ask yourself, "Who does what?" The answer should be the sentence subject.

EXAMPLE: The employees of Do Nuttin' Bakery often play coed softball games, and ______________________________.
(usually a good time is had by everyone)

SOLUTION: The employees of Do Nuttin' Bakery often play coed softball games, and usually everyone has a good time.

1. But two teams gathered at Rough Diamond Park on a Sunday afternoon, and

   ______________________________.
   (trouble was gotten into by everyone)

2. The pitcher, Mary, hit the batter, Tina, with a wild pitch, and

   ______________________________.
   (the ball was thrown back at Mary by Tina)

3. Tina's teammates charged from the dugout, and

   ______________________________.
   (home plate was surrounded by Mary's teammates)

4. Tina's team claimed that Mary hit Tina on purpose, but

   ______________________________.
   (it was argued by Mary's team that a new pitch was just being tried out by Mary)

5. Finally, Mary demonstrated her new pitch, so

    ____.
    (it could be seen by everyone why control of the ball was lost by Mary)

6. Mary pitched an impressive curve ball, but

    ____.
    (the ball wasn't pitched over home plate by her)

Exercise Two Exam Stress

Sigmund, a college student, is taking an exam in his psychology class, and one of his short-essay questions reads:

What are some of the causes of problems between parents and teenagers?

Immediately Sigmund writes down some points he wants to include in his answer:

1. Rules and expectations aren't made clear.
2. Resentment occurs when chores aren't done.
3. Blame is placed on teenagers for anything that goes wrong in the home.
4. The way in which parents discipline is by yelling too much.
5. The complaint is that teenagers aren't listened to.
6. There isn't the recognition that parents are human beings too.
7. Enough respect isn't shown to parents.

Then Sigmund begins to write his answer:

"The causes of problems between parents and teenagers are . . ."

But he gets stuck before he even begins to show what he knows. Why? He has begun by focusing his first sentence on the subject causes, an abstract word, and the verb *are*. It looks like he is going to name <u>all</u> of the causes of problems in one sentence.

Help Sigmund by writing a more clearly focused beginning sentence. Ask yourself, "Who does what?" and make your answer the subject of the sentence.

Write your beginning sentence here:

____

____

Now go back and improve the focus of six of the seven sentences in Sigmund's notes. Ask yourself, "Who does what?" in each sentence, and make your answer the sentence subject. Write your clearly focused sentences in the spaces provided. Sigmund's original sentences appear in parentheses below the spaces.

EXAMPLE 1: (Rules and expectations aren't made clear.)

SOLUTION: Parents don't make their rules and expectations clear.

2. ______________________________
(Resentment occurs when chores aren't done.)

3. ______________________________
(Blame is placed on teenagers for anything that goes wrong in the home.)

4. ______________________________
(The way in which parents discipline is by yelling too much.)

5. ______________________________
(The complaint is that teenagers aren't listened to.)

6. ______________________________
(There isn't the recognition by teenagers that parents are human beings too.)

7. ______________________________
(Enough respect isn't shown to parents.)

Now write three well-focused sentences in which you state what you think are the causes of conflict between teenagers and parents:

1. ______________________________
____

2. ______________________________
____

3. ______________________________
____

Exercise Three Who's to Blame?

Applying what you know about focusing sentences, we now go back to the paragraph about Professor Seed and clarify the focus of the sentences in the paragraph. The original, unfocused sentences are given in parentheses. Ask yourself, "Who does what?" and make your answer the sentence subject.

EXAMPLE a. ______________________________

(The way in which he set his alarm clock was incorrect.)

SOLUTION: He incorrectly set his alarm clock.

b. ______________________________

(so the early bus was missed and campus wasn't reached until 30 minutes after his first class began.)

c. ______________________________

(Then the classroom couldn't be found.)

d. ______________________________

(Help was given by many students,)

e. ______________________________

(but still the wrong classroom was appeared at by him.)

f. ______________________________

(Finally the realization came that his wallet was lost,)

g. ______________________________

(so bus fare had to be borrowed.)

h. ______________________________

____

(At home that night, he was told by his wife that the reason he had a bad day was because the wrong foot was started off on.)

Exercise Four The Farmer's Market

Are the following sentences written in active or passive voice? After you decide, rewrite the following the sentences that are written in the passive voice so that they are active.

1. Every week, I shop at our local farmer's market.

 ____

2. The kale, one of my favorite farm's specialties, is loved by me.

 ____

3. My sister loves the canteloupe.

 ____

4. The carrots are grown by the Woodstock farmer.

 ____

5. My mother is driven to the market by me every week.

 ____

6. I always bring my own bags when I shop.

 ____

7. The corn is dropped off by the grower's son.

 ____

Unit Four

Joining Sentences with Coordinators

When your sentences are clearly focused, you'll find it much easier to join sentences that are logically related. In this unit, you will practice using the seven coordinators. The easiest way to remember them is to remember the word *FANBOYS*, which is an acronym, a word made up of the first letters of the names of the seven coordinators. In the example sentences below, notice the logical relationships that the coordinators express:

	Coordinators	**Logical Relationships**
For:	Mary enjoys math, for it is challenging.	effect/cause
And:	Thuy has won several trophies, and she is an honor student.	addition
Nor:	Judy doesn't work, nor does she want a job.	addition of negatives
But:	Nabil is pretty good at gymnastics, but he prefers gymnastics.	contrast
Or:	Jaime needs a vacation, or he'll go crazy.	alternative
Yet:	Irma doesn't earn much, yet she spends money like a millionaire.	contrast
So:	The coach praised the team excessively, so the players stopped believing him.	cause/effect

PUNCTUATION: When coordinators join sentences, commas come before the coordinators, following this pattern: *sentence + comma + coordinator + sentence*.

The coordinators are important because:

1. We can use them to join sentences, which helps eliminate choppiness in our writing.

2. Unlike other joining words, they can also show logical relationships between two separate sentences; we can begin sentences with coordinators.

   Siu Fong practiced gymnastics every day. So she eventually excelled at it.

3. Most importantly, the coordinators help to express logical relationships between sentences.

Exercise One Old House

Join the following sets of sentences, using coordinators. The logical relationships are given in brackets.

EXAMPLE: Most people want to own their own home.
They can't afford one. *[contrast]*

SOLUTION: Most people want to own their own home, but they can't afford one.

1. Sid and Sal found an old, inexpensive house they could afford.
They bought it. *[cause/effect]*

2. They wanted a newer house.
New houses were too costly. *[contrast]*

3. Sid and Sal applied for a loan to fix up the dilapidated building.
The lender approved it. *[addition]*

4. They replaced the old toilet in the upstairs bathroom.
The bathtub fell through the rotted floor into the kitchen below. *[contrast]*

5. They were not pleased to find a hornet's nest in the attic.
They were not happy to find termites in the foundation. *[addition of negatives]*

6. The house was in danger of collapsing any day.
   The termites had devoured most of the foundation. *[effect/cause]*

7. Sid and Sal decided they should jack up the house
   to replace the foundation.
   Their house would be a "goner." *[alternative]*

8. The construction workers had to work on the foundation.
   They lifted the house gently with hydraulic jacks. *[cause/effect]*

9. The crew completed the foundation.
   The roof caved in. *[contrast]*

10. Sid and Sal now enjoy living in the backyard.
    It's a lot safer than living in their house. *[effect/cause]*

Exercise Two Buying a Laptop

Join the following sentences, again using the coordinators; this time you will choose the coordinators that best show the logical relationships.

EXAMPLE: Maria decided to buy a new laptop.
She didn't know much about laptops.

SOLUTION: Maria decided to buy a new laptop, but (or yet) she didn't know much about laptops.

1. She wanted to be a well-informed shopper.
   She began to do research.

2. She did a lot of online research.
   She even found consumer reports on popular laptops.

3. She didn't consider laptop computers.
   She needed a larger screen.

4. She was attracted to the 15-inch model.
   The 15-inch was heavier than she wanted.

5. The most affordable laptop for Maria was the Mango Pro.
   The laptop's consumer rating was "Extremely Poor."

6. A more expensive laptop was rated favorably in the consumer reports.
   It had an additional warranty for repairs.

7. Maria needed to test several laptops.
   She would not know if they had the features she needed.

8. The salesperson for TechnoGeek did not treat Maria courteously.
   The overpriced TechnoGeek laptops did not impress her.

9. The salesperson selling the economical FlexiComp laptop treated
   Maria with respect.
   She left the store with a brand-new FlexiComp laptop.

10. Maria is happy with her new laptop.
    She still wishes she had a much bigger screen.

Exercise Three You Be the Co-Author

Complete the following sentences by filling in the blank spaces with information that relates to your life and that logically fits with the coordinators given. Note: You'll have the chance to use all of the seven coordinators or *fanboys*: *for*, *and*, *nor*, *but*, *or*, *yet*, and *so*.

1. I wanted to choose a suitable career for myself, so ____________________

   ____.

2. I considered ______________, but ____________________
   Name a profession.

   ____.

3. I talked to ____________________ about possible careers, and ____________
   Name a person or people.

   ____.

4. I knew I didn't want to be a ______________, nor ______________

   ____.

5. The profession of ____________________ seemed appealing to me, for ________

   ____.

6. My parents think I should be a ______________, yet ______________

   ____.

7. Now I think I should ______________, or ______________

   ____.

Unit Five

Joining Sentences with Subordinators

Subordinators are sentence-joining words that, like the coordinators, help us show a variety of relationships between ideas. Here are the subordinators we use most often:

Subordinator	Logical Relationship	Example
although, though, even though, while, whereas	contrast	Although I am a senior, I have 40 more units to take.
because, since	effect/cause	School is taking longer because I have to work.
if	condition	I can go to the movies if I finish my homework.
unless	condition	I cannot go to the movies unless I finish my homework. (*Unless I finish* means *if I don't finish*.)
before, after, when, whenever, until, as soon as	time	After I finish my homework, I'll go to the movies.

When we put a subordinator in front of a sentence, we change the sentence from an independent clause to a dependent (or subordinate) clause. A dependent clause cannot be a sentence by itself, so we have to join it to an independent clause:

Because she purchased her ticket in advance, *(dependent clause)*
she got a discount fare. *(independent clause)*

She got a discount fare *(independent clause)*
because she purchased her ticket in advance. *(dependent clause)*

Here is the rule to remember when using the subordinators to join two logically related ideas:

The dependent clause can come first or second in the sentence, but the two logically related ideas must appear in the same sentence.

She bought a ticket in advance. ***(sentence)***
Because she bought a ticket in advance. ***(fragment, not a sentence)***
Because she bought a ticket in advance, she got a discount fare. ***(sentence)***

PUNCTUATION: When the subordinate clause comes first in a sentence, it is followed by a comma, following this pattern: *subordinate clause* + *comma* + *independent clause*.

Exercise One Infotainment

Combine the following pairs of sentences using subordinators. Make the underlined sentence into the subordinate, or dependent, clause; the logical relationship is given in brackets. (Hint: Read the whole exercise before combining the sentence sets.)

EXAMPLE: Some talk shows discuss current events.
Ginny watches them to be entertained. *[contrast]*

SOLUTION: Although some talk shows discuss current events, Ginny watches them to be entertained.

1. Ginny likes to watch shows that cover current events mixed with celebrity gossip.
   She prefers shows that cover a variety of topics. *[cause/effect]*

2. Ginny thinks it's acceptable to learn about the day's events through talk shows.
   Andres prefers to read the paper to keep current on local and national news. *[contrast]*

3. Ginny gets her news only from entertaining talk shows.
   She is very well informed. *[contrast]*

4. There is a big story.
   Current events are reported before celebrity gossip. *[condition]*

5. There are no fascinating political stories.
Reporters focus entirely on celebrity news. ***[condition]***

6. Most people don't like the paparazzi.
They submit the best celebrity photos for stories on the shows Ginny watches. ***[condition]***

7. Ginny will continue watching infotainment programs.
She thinks she gets the best coverage of the day's events. ***[cause/effect]***

Exercise Two Urban Green

In the following exercise, first decide how the ideas in the two separate sentences are logically related; then, choose a subordinator that shows the relationship and use it to join the two sentences.

EXAMPLE: Urban policymakers need to take action.
The number of trees in American cities has decreased by 25 percent in the last 25 years.

SOLUTION: Urban policymakers need to take action because the number of trees in American cities has decreased by 25 percent in the last 25 years.

1. Fires and diseases have caused American cities to lose trees.
They are not the main cause of tree loss.

2. Cities experience the most tree loss.
Trees are removed for office buildings, shopping malls, homes, and parking lots.

3. Some people claim that trees take up too much space in urban areas.
A significant body of research shows the benefits of trees to the environment and human health.

4. Trees clean the environment.
They filter pollutants from the air and water.

5. Sick people recover faster.
   They recuperate around trees.

6. Children have spent time in nature.
   They pay more attention.

7. Research suggests that people want to exercise more.
   They are surrounded by greenery.

8. Some people argue that the government shouldn't take action.
   It needs to solve other problems first, such as urban crime.

9. But studies show that people are less aggressive.
   They live near trees.

10. City governments begin to sponsor tree-planting for residents.
    They will continue to lose trees and their benefits.

Exercise Three You Be the Co-Author

Complete the following sentences by filling in the blanks with subordinate clauses beginning with the subordinators given or with main clauses. Be sure to add information that relates to your own life and that logically fits with the given subordinator.

1. Next summer, I want to travel because ______________________________

   ____.

2. I'm considering going to __________ although ______________________________
   (Name a place.)

   ____.

3. I dream of going to __________ whenever ______________________________
   (Name a place.)

   ____.

4. While Spain sounds exciting, ____________________ is more affordable.
   (Name a place.)

5. I can't go anywhere unless ______________________________.

6. Before ______________________________,
   I might have to renew my passport.

7. When I asked my closest friend for suggestions, he (or she) ____________________

   ____.

8. Even though I was offered a summer job, ______________________________.

9. After thinking it over, I've decided to ______________________________

   because ______________________________.

10. I would travel around the world if ______________________________

    ______________________________.

Joining Words That Show Logical Relationships

Relationship	Coordinators	Subordinators
Addition	and nor	
Cause/Effect	so	
Effect/Cause	for	because since as
Contrast	but yet	although even though though while whereas
Concession		although even though though while whereas
Alternative	or	
Condition		if whether unless
Time		after before since until while when whenever as soon as

Coordinators can (1) join sentences or (2) introduce complete sentences.

1. Lucy has a new computer, but she doesn't know how to use it.
2. Lucy has a new computer. But she doesn't know how to use it.

Subordinators can (1) join sentences or (2) introduce sentences if the clauses they are attached to are followed by commas and then by independent clauses.

1. Kevin likes his job because he makes a lot of money.
2. Because he makes a lot of money, Kevin likes his job.

In the following review exercise, you will use coordinators and subordinators to join sentences and show logical relationships. In some sets, you are asked to join first with a coordinator and then with a subordinator. (Refer to the chart on page 65 for help.)

EXAMPLE: Many people can't seem to live without chocolate.
Scientists wonder if chocolate is addictive.

SOLUTION 1: Many people can't seem to live without chocolate, so scientists wonder if chocolate is addictive. ***(coordinator)***

SOLUTION 2: Scientists wonder if chocolate is addictive, for many people can't seem to live without it. ***(coordinator)***

SOLUTION 3: Because many people can't seem to live without chocolate, scientists wonder if it is addictive. ***(subordinator)***

1. There are many delicious kinds of chocolate.
Milk chocolate is the most popular kind in the United States.

    a. Use a coordinator:

    ____

    ____

    b. Use a subordinator:

    ____

    ____

2. The average American consumes ten pounds of chocolate every year.
This number is increasing.

    a. Use a coordinator:

    ____

    ____

3. Some of us get hooked on chocolate.
The chemicals in chocolate can help us feel good.

    a. Use a coordinator:

    ____

    ____

    b. Use a subordinator:

    ____

    ____

4. Pyrazines in chocolate attract humans.
   Pyrazines smell good.

   a. Use a coordinator:

   ____

   ____

   b. Use a subordinator:

   ____

   ____

5. The chemical phenylethylamine in chocolate appeals to chocolate lovers.
   It gets people out of sad moods.

   a. Use a coordinator:

   ____

   ____

   b. Use a subordinator:

   ____

   ____

6. People consume carbohydrates, a component of chocolate.
   Their moods improve and they feel more alert.

   a. Use a subordinator:

   ____

   ____

7. We can eat chocolate to get all the benefits.
   We might gain weight.

   a. Use a coordinator:

   ____

   ____

   b. Use a subordinator:

   ____

   ____

8. People think that they are addicted to chocolate.
   They have two choices.

   a. Use a subordinator:

   ____

   ____

9. They can quit eating chocolate altogether.
   They can try to eat less.

   a. Use a coordinator:

   ____

   ____

10. Many people won't give up their chocolate habit.
    They can't imagine a life without chocolate.

    a. Use a coordinator:

    ____

    ____

    b. Use a subordinator:

    ____

    ____

Unit Six

Joining Sentences to Show Comparison and Contrast

In your college courses, and in your personal lives and professional careers as well, you will frequently compare and contrast people, things, or ideas. Employers often must compare and contrast two or more job applicants, college students may compare and contrast two historical periods, and people often compare and contrast two products they are considering buying or two people they know. By joining ideas or information with coordinators and subordinators, you can clearly show similarities and differences to your reader.

For example, because two college freshmen, George and Paul, are twin brothers, we expect them to be similar, but they are actually different in some ways. Here are random lists of information we have gathered about them:

George

is tall and slim
likes to read science fiction
runs three miles daily
has brown eyes and brown hair
works as a cartographer's assistant 15 hours per week
is an engineering major

Paul

has brown eyes and brown hair
is tall and slim
still hasn't found a major
likes to read poetry
hates to exercise
works 20 hours per week as an usher in a theater

The above information about the twins is not listed in any organized way. So, after we gather information about two subjects (in this case, the twins), the next step toward comparing and contrasting them is to organize the lists according to related points, here the twins' physical descriptions, interests, jobs, and college majors:

George

has brown hair and brown eyes
is tall and slim
likes to read science fiction
runs three miles daily
works as a cartographer's assistant 15 hours per week
is an engineering major

Paul

has brown hair and brown eyes
is tall and slim
likes to read poetry
hates to exercise
works as an usher in a theater 20 hours per week
still hasn't found a major

We can now express the similarities and differences between the twins in sentences using the coordinators and subordinators that you reviewed in Units Four and Five.

Exercise One George and Paul

The following sentences express the similarities and differences between the twins, George and Paul. In each sentence, circle the joining word(s) that show comparison or contrast and then list the words you've circled.

1. Both George and Paul have brown eyes and brown hair.
2. George and Paul both are tall and slim.
3. George likes to read science fiction, but Paul likes to read poetry.
4. George runs three miles daily, yet Paul hates to exercise.
5. While George works as a cartographer's assistant 15 hours per week, Paul works as an usher in a theater 20 hours per week.
6. Although George is an engineering major, Paul still hasn't found a major.

Comparison Words **Contrast Words**

In addition to showing the similarities and differences between people, we often compare and contrast behavior, cultures, theories, points of view on an issue, the positive and negative features of something, or the past with the present. The exercises in this unit give you practice in using coordinators and subordinators to compare and contrast activities, cultures, and a past and present condition. The following chart summarizes the joining words that show the logical relationships of comparison and contrast.

Summary of Comparison and Contrast Joining Words

	Comparison	Contrast
Coordinators	and	but, yet
Subordinators		although even though though while whereas

Coordinators can join sentences and begin sentences. When they join sentences, place a comma before the coordinator.

Kim likes heavy metal, but Tom prefers classical music.
Kim likes heavy metal. But Tom prefers classical music.

Subordinators join dependent clauses to sentences. When the dependent clause comes first, place a comma after it; if the dependent clause follows the independent clause, don't use a comma.

While Kim likes prime rib, Tom prefers rice and vegetables.
Kim likes prime rib while Tom prefers rice and vegetables.

Exercise Two Moving Out

Diana is graduating from college and is ready to move to her own place. To make a rational choice and one that fits her lifestyle, she lists what she should know about living in both the city and the country:

Country Living	**City Living**
is quiet and relaxing	can be exciting and lively
offers cheaper rents	provides more restaurants and nightlife
moves family closer	moves her closer to other family members
offers larger rental apartments	has more modern conveniences
provides parking	provides parking

Step 1: Organize the two lists according to related points:

Country Living	**City Living**
1. is quiet and relaxing	can be exciting and lively
2.	
3.	
4.	
5.	

Step 2: Using the coordinators *and*, *but*, and *yet*, and the subordinators *while*, *whereas*, *although*, *even though*, and *though*, write five sentences in which you compare and contrast country and city living, using the information you organized in Step 1.

1.

2.

3.

4.

5.

Exercise Three The Nuer and the Bakhteri

In this exercise, you will compare and contrast two cultures—the Nuer and the Bakhteri. Here are random lists of information about the two cultures:

The Nuer

are pastoral people
divide labor according to sex
occupy a flat, grassy region
use products from cattle for shelter and food
live in the Sudan
raise dairy cattle
women herd the cattle

The Bakhteri

men herd the sheep and goats
live in Southern Iran
are pastoral people
raise sheep and goats
divide labor according to sex
occupy a mountainous area
use products from sheep and goats for shelter and food

Step 1: Complete the following lists by organizing the information according to related points.

The Nuer	The Bakhteri
1. are pastoral people	are pastoral people
2. live in the Sudan	live in Southern Iran
3.	
4.	
5.	
6.	
7.	

Step 2: Write sentences in which you join related similarities and differences using the coordinators and subordinators that show comparison and contrast. Follow the examples below.

1. Both the Nuer and the Bakhteri are pastoral people.

2. The Nuer live in the Sudan while the Bakhteri live in Southern Iran.

   You should create five more sentences from your lists in Step 1. Be sure to use a variety of coordinators and subordinators that show contrast.

3.

4.

5.

6.

7.

Exercise Four The Netsilik and the Trobriands

Following the two steps you took in Exercises Two and Three, compare and contrast two cultures—the Netsilik and the Trobriands. Organize the lists, then write six sentences using joining words that show comparison and contrast.

The Netsilik

hunt seals and caribou
occupy a cold desert environment
live on the Arctic coast

migrate seasonally
build houses of snow and ice

value the extended family

The Trobriands

live in villages all year
value the extended family
are horticulturists whose primary crop is yams
occupy warm coral islands
live on the Trobriand Islands off the coast of New Guinea
build wooden houses clustered in small villages

Step 1: Organize the lists.

1.

2.

3.

4.

5.

6.

Step 2: Combine related points into sentences using coordinators and subordinators. Be sure to use a variety of coordinators and subordinators that show contrast.

1.

2.

3.

4.

5.

6.

Comparing the Present and the Past

While attending her 25-year high school reunion, Jonita saw her old boyfriend Peter, whom she hadn't seen since graduation. She was surprised by the changes in him, and wrote a letter to her best friend describing the changes:

> Peter has changed a great deal in the last 25 years. Although Peter had curly red hair 25 years ago, he now has almost no hair at all. While he once played basketball, now he just watches sports on TV. He hated to read in school, but now he reads all the time. In high school, he wanted to be an engineer, but today he teaches history at a junior college. Most importantly, in high school, he vowed to stay single forever, yet now he is a married man with two children.

When we compare and contrast the past with the present, we have to be careful of verb tenses so that the time is clear for our readers. Notice that Jonita uses the past tense forms of verbs to describe Peter's condition 25 years ago and present tense forms of verbs to describe the way he is now. Watch for time words that indicate which tense should be used:

Time	Past Tense	*Time*	Present Tense
25 years ago	had curly red hair	Now	has almost no hair
Once	played	Now	watches
in school	hated	Now	reads
in high school	wanted	Today	teaches
Once	vowed	Now	is

Exercise Five The Middleton Boom

In the following paragraph, fill in each blank with the correct tense of the given verb. Notice that the topic sentence makes it clear that the paragraph will show the differences between Middleton in the past and Middleton now. (It helps to skim the entire passage before filling in the blanks.)

The town of Middleton has changed a great deal in 30 years. Thirty years ago, its population ___________ (be) 3,000, while now it ___________ (be) 43,000. Many of the current residents now ___________ (work) in the insurance business, a business that ___________ (do) not exist until 1980, when Pay Up Insurance Company ___________ (establish) its headquarters there. Immediately the insurance business ___________ (attract) unemployed workers from all over the state who in turn ___________ (create) the need for new services. Before 1980, Middleton ___________ (have) no libraries, yet now it ___________ (have) three, each adjacent to new high schools, which ___________ (be) built within a three-year period from 1985 to 1988. Students graduating from middle school formerly ___________ (go) to high school in a neighboring town, but now they ___________ (attend) school in their hometown.

Exercise Six Life in the Early 1900s

In the following paragraph, fill in each blank with the correct tense of the given verb. Like in the exercise in page 85, the topic sentence makes it clear that the paragraph will show the differences between life in the early 1900s and life today. Make sure to skim the entire passage before beginning to fill in the blanks.

In many ways, life today ______________ (be) much easier than it ______________ (be) in the early 1900s. Over a hundred years ago, people ______________ (live) in either the city or the country. Today, there ______________ (is) sprawling suburbs between cities and rural areas. People also ______________ (work) at businesses that ______________ (is) not in their towns; in the early 1900s, most people ______________ (work) right where they ______________ (live). It goes without saying that technology did not ______________ (exist); the telephone ______________ (is) ______________ (still) (consider) a new device that not many people ______________ (have). In your opinion, ______________ (be) life better or worse than it ______________ (is) a hundred years ago?

Unit Seven

Joining Sentences to Show Concession

What is concession? In everyday life, to concede means to reluctantly accept that something is true. In grammar, however, concession signals a relationship between ideas in a sentence and generally suggests something opposite of the main part of the sentence. For instance, you could say, "Although my dog growls, she's really very friendly and sweet" as a way to show concession. The dog may growl, but underneath that gruffness is a sweet animal who doesn't bite. That idea was conveyed in the sentence.

Words that indicate concession are *despite*, *nevertheless*, and *although*, to name a few. Keep that in mind as you do the exercises in this chapter and learn more about concession.

Exercise One Pets Do the Strangest Things

Join the following sentences so that they make one sentence that expresses concession.

1. My cat is starving in the morning.
   He won't eat if he is alone in the kitchen.

2. My dog is lazy.
   She loves to play fetch for hours.

3. I bathe my dog twice a week.
   She always smells bad.

4. I got my pets so I wouldn't be lonely.
   They often hide from me.

5. My cat loves loud music.
   He runs when he hears thunder.

Exercise Two The Star Quarterbacks

Read the following short paragraphs and follow the directions given under each of them.

1. Both Hunk and Rabbit are star quarterbacks. They both play for the Middleton Marvels, and both have been invaluable players. Hunk is fast and strong, and Rabbit is too.

Circle the joining words and list them here:

2. Both Hunk and Rabbit are star quarterbacks, but they have different strengths. Hunk has had more experience in pro football, but Rabbit is young and learns quickly. Rabbit has a strong arm and executes long passes well, yet Hunk is precise on short- and medium-range passes. Rabbit is fast, but Hunk can make quick decisions on the line of scrimmage.

Circle the joining words and list them here:

3. Although Hunk and Rabbit are star quarterbacks, they have different strengths. While Rabbit is young and learns quickly, Hunk has had more experience in pro football. Even though Rabbit has a strong arm and throws long passes well, Hunk is precise on short- and medium-range passes. Whereas Rabbit is fast, Hunk can make quick decisions on the line of scrimmage.

Circle the joining words and list them here:

After reading paragraph 3, do you have the sense that the writer thinks one player is better than the other? Which one? Why?

The Concessive Subordinators

As we discussed at the beginning of the unit, we use words like *although*, *even though*, *though*, *while*, and *whereas* to show contrast. These are called *contrast* subordinators. But they do more than just show contrast: They **de-emphasize** the points they are attached to and, at the same time, show **concession**. When we concede a point, we admit that it has value. Concessive subordinators are highly useful in presenting written arguments because they allow us to concede, or admit, that an opposing point has merit and, at the same time, to de-emphasize the opposing point's importance to the reader.

For e.g., football fans in the town of Middleton disagree about who the starting quarterback on the Middleton Marvels should be—Hunk or Rabbit. The local newspaper has invited readers to submit their opinions in letters to the editor.

A fan in favor of Hunk writes:

> Although Rabbit has a strong arm and executes long passes well, Hunk is precise on short- and medium-range passes, so he should be the starting quarterback.

A fan in favor of Rabbit writes:

> Although Hunk is precise on short- and medium-range passes, Rabbit has a strong arm and executes long passes well, so he should be the starting quarterback.

Using the same information about the two quarterbacks, both fans have used *although*, not only to contrast the two players, but also to concede that the competitor does have good points; at the same time, the writers de-emphasize the competitor's good points. (The fans could also use the subordinators *while* and *whereas*, but *although*, *even though*, and *though* are the strongest concessive subordinators.)

Conceding a point shows that we acknowledge that an issue is complex and that in forming our opinion, we have considered the opposition. People who read an opinion that merely states "Rabbit has a strong arm and executes long passes well, so he should be the starting quarterback" will wonder "But what about Hunk's precision on short- and medium-range passes?" and will be less likely to value the writer's opinion.

Summary of Contrast and Concession Words

	CONTRAST	CONCESSION
COORDINATORS	but, yet	
SUBORDINATORS	although	although
	even though	even though
	though	though
	while	while
	whereas	whereas

Choosing Contrast Coordinators or Subordinators

Coordinators give equal emphasis to the ideas they join.

Subordinators de-emphasize the ideas they are attached to.

Punctuation Reminders: Using Commas

When joining sentences with coordinators:
Add a comma before the coordinator.

Elisa bought a car, but she doesn't know how to drive.

When joining sentences with subordinators:
Add a comma after the subordinate clause if it comes first in the sentence.

Although Elisa doesn't know how to drive, she bought a car.

Don't add a comma if the main clause comes first:

Elisa bought a car although she doesn't know how to drive.

Practice in Contrast and Concession: Two Neighborhoods

We often move to new locations because we are leaving home to go away to school, taking a new job, buying a home to accommodate a growing family, or retiring to a place more hospitable to the elderly. Whatever our reasons for moving, we try to find a neighborhood that will best suit our needs and lifestyles.

In the following exercise, you will be contrasting two neighborhoods in Marina City, or contrasting one neighborhood's advantage with a disadvantage. You will be either joining two sentences to simply show contrast or joining two sentences to show contrast and concession and to emphasize information about one neighborhood.

Remember that the coordinators *but* and *yet* show contrast, giving equal emphasis to the ideas they join, while the subordinators *although*, *even though*, *though*, *while*, and *whereas* show contrast and concession, de-emphasizing the points they are attached to.

Directions for joining are given in italics.

EXAMPLE 1: Sunny Hills is close to public transportation.
Sea View is near a beautiful park.

a. *Show contrast; give equal emphasis:*

SOLUTION: Sunny Hills is close to public transportation, but Sea View is near a beautiful park.

EXPLANATION: To give equal emphasis to the good features of the two neighborhoods, we use the coordinator *but* (or *yet*) to join and contrast the two sentences.

b. *Show concession; emphasize the good point of Sea View:*

SOLUTION: Although Sunny Hills is close to public transportation, Sea View is near a beautiful park.

EXPLANATION: We emphasize the good feature of Sea View by placing the concessive subordinator *although* before the information about Sunny Hills. We admit that Sunny Hills has a good feature, but we emphasize the good feature of Sea View.

EXAMPLE 2: Sea View is near a beautiful park.
Sea View is far from the college campus.

a. Show contrast; give equal emphasis:

SOLUTION: Sea View is near a beautiful park, yet it is far from the college campus.

b. Show concession; emphasize the distance from campus:

SOLUTION: Even though Sea View is near a beautiful park, it is far from the college campus.

Exercise Three Sunny Hills and Sea View

1. Sea View is close to a museum.
   Sunny Hills has its own swimming pool and bike paths.

   a. *Show contrast and give equal emphasis:*

   ____

   ____

   b. *Show concession and emphasize the advantage of Sea View:*

   ____

   ____

2. Sunny Hills is close to the college campus.
   Sunny Hills has limited parking.

   a. *Show concession and emphasize a disadvantage of Sunny Hills:*

   ____

   ____

   b. *Show concession and emphasize an advantage of Sunny Hills:*

   ____

   ____

3. Sunny Hills is close to a shopping mall.
   Sea View has many small shops and cafes.

   a. *Show contrast and give equal emphasis:*

   ____

   ____

   b. *Show concession and emphasize a good feature of Sea View:*

   ____

   ____

Exercise Four My Neighborhood

In the following exercise, you will join sentences to show people's points of view about their neighborhoods, using the concessive subordinators *although*, *even though*, *though*, *while*, and *whereas* to concede a point and, at the same time, to de-emphasize it while emphasizing what's important to the resident.

Directions are given in italics; choose the most important information to emphasize by identifying what is most important to the resident named in the directions.

EXAMPLE: Sea View has no nightclubs or dance spots.
Sea View is close to the city's main library.

a. *Join from the point of view of a college student who loves to party more than study:*

SOLUTION: While Sea View is close to the city's main library, it has no nightclubs or dance spots.

b. *Join from the point of view of a college student whose first priority is doing research:*

SOLUTION: Although Sea View has no nightclubs or dance spots, it is close to the city's main library.

1. Sea View has two great cafes.
Sea View is far from campus.

a. *Join from the point of view of a college student without a car, whose most important concern is having a way to get to school:*

____

____

b. *Join from the point of view of a professor with a car whose day isn't complete unless she has her morning espresso at a local cafe:*

____

____

2. Sunny Hills has several outstanding public schools.
Sunny Hills has an excellent private school.

a. *Join from the point of view of a parent of two children in public schools:*

____

____

b. *Join from the point of view of a parent of two children in private school:*

3. Sea View has poor public transportation.
   Sea View has many services for senior citizens.

   a. *Join from the point of view of a retired man in his 70s:*

   b. *Join from the point of view of a woman who rides the bus to work:*

4. Sea View has great ocean views.
   Sea View is far from the freeway.

   a. *Join from the point of view of a computer specialist who must commute by freeway daily:*

   b. *Join from the point of view of a person who rarely leaves home:*

5. Sunny Hills has an outdoor swimming pool and bike paths.
   Sunny Hills has no fitness centers.

   a. *Join from the point of view of a person who is physically active:*

   b. *Join from the point of view of a guy who likes to lift weights in front of an admiring audience:*

6. Sunny Hills has many neighborhood problems.
   Sunny Hills has active community organizations.

   a. *Join from the point of view of a resident who'd just like peace and quiet:*

   ____

   ____

   b. *Join from the point of view of a community activist who loves working for a good cause:*

   ____

   ____

Practice in Contrast and Concession: Alternatives to Gasoline

Most vehicles in the United States use only gasoline and diesel, both made from oil. To reduce pollution, transportation costs, and dependence on imported oil, U.S. government regulators, automakers, and consumers are considering alternative fuels. Take a look at the following chart, which lists the advantages and disadvantages of different alternative fuels, because it contains information that you will use in sentence combining in Exercises Three and Four.

Contrasting the Fuel Alternatives

	Advantages	Disadvantages
Gasoline	available everywhere technology in place	pollutes the environment unreliable foreign sources
100% Biodiesel	domestically produced made from renewable plant and animal sources	limited availability expensive sources
Electricity	produces zero emissions car batteries rechargeable at home	made at polluting power plants long recharging times
Hydrogen Gas	almost pollution free produced from renewable natural gas resources	costly to produce and distribute difficult to fit large fuel tanks on cars
Compressed Natural Gas	comes from vast domestic gas reserves clean burning, non-petroleum	difficult to fit large fuel tanks on cars long tank-filling times

In the following exercise, you will join sentences using the coordinators *but* and *yet* to contrast fuels and give equal emphasis, and you will use the subordinators *although*, *even though*, *though*, *while*, and *whereas* not only to contrast fuels but also to emphasize a point and show concession.

You will see two sentences, followed by directions for joining them given in italics.

EXAMPLE: Compressed natural gas comes from vast domestic gas reserves. Biodiesel is made from renewable plant and animal sources.

a. Show contrast; give equal emphasis:

SOLUTION: Compressed natural gas comes from vast domestic gas reserves, but biodiesel is made from renewable plant and animal sources.

EXPLANATION: Here we joined the two sentences with the coordinator *but* (or *yet*) to simply contrast the two fuels and give equal emphasis to their advantages.

b. Show concession; emphasize the advantage of compressed natural gas:

SOLUTION: Although biodiesel is made from renewable plant and animal sources, compressed natural gas comes from vast domestic gas reserves.

EXPLANATION: To emphasize the advantage of compressed natural gas, we placed the concessive subordinator *although* in front of the sentence about biodiesel. Now we have de-emphasized the advantage of biodiesel and emphasized the advantage of compressed natural gas. At the same time, we joined the two sentences, showed contrast, and conceded, or admitted, that biodiesel does have a good quality.

Exercise Five Alternatives to Gasoline

Join the following sets of sentences, following the directions given in italics. Remember that coordinators and subordinators both show contrast, but the coordinators *but* and *yet* give equal emphasis to the sentences they join, and the subordinators *although*, *even though*, *though*, *while*, and *whereas* de-emphasize the ideas they are attached to. Refer to the previous page for examples.

1. Gasoline is available everywhere.
   Electric car batteries are rechargeable at home.

   a. *Show contrast and give equal emphasis:*

   ____

   ____

   b. *Show concession and emphasize the advantage of gasoline:*

   ____

   ____

2. Electricity requires long recharging times.
   Compressed natural gas requires long tank-filling times.

   a. *Show concession and emphasize the disadvantage of compressed natural gas:*

   ____

   ____

3. Electricity produces zero emissions.
   Electricity is made at polluting power plants.

   a. *Show concession and emphasize electricity's good point:*

   ____

   ____

4. Biodiesel is made from renewable plant and animal sources.
   These sources are expensive.

   a. *Show concession; emphasize the disadvantage of biodiesel:*

   ____

   ____

Exercise Six Taking a Stand

From the chart on page 105, choose the fuel that you think is best, and state your opinion in a sentence here:

Using information from the chart, complete the following:

1. Write a sentence in which you concede, or admit, an advantage of another fuel while emphasizing an advantage of your fuel:

   ____

   ____

2. Write a sentence in which you concede a disadvantage of your fuel and emphasize a disadvantage of another fuel:

   ____

   ____

3. Write a sentence in which you concede a disadvantage of your fuel and emphasize one of its advantages:

   ____

   ____

4. Consider the pollution that can be generated in a car using your fuel.

   If your fuel pollutes the environment, write a sentence in which you concede the pollution problem while emphasizing an advantage of your fuel:

   ____

   ____

   If your fuel does not pollute the environment, write a sentence in which you concede a disadvantage of your fuel and emphasize the fact that it doesn't pollute:

   ____

   ____

Unit Eight

Showing Logical Relationships with Transition Words

In addition to the two categories of joining words you've studied—coordinators and subordinators—we have another category of words that show logical relationships between ideas—**transition words**, such as *however* and *therefore*. Unlike coordinators and subordinators, transition words do not join sentences.

To see how writers use transition words, you can skim through published writing, looking for transition words. But you'll discover that they are hard to find because writers use them sparingly, mainly to show relationships or make connections between idea units, or sets of ideas, while using coordinators and subordinators more frequently to join sentences.

Using Transition Words Effectively

Here is an example of transition words used effectively in writing:

> Is reality TV really "real"? Some say it is, but I disagree. **For example**, how real is it for 16 people to be dropped on a desert island with no food, water, or sunscreen and be able to survive? In my opinion, without help from the producers, they would get badly sunburned and starve to death. That's not real. **Similarly**, "housewives" are people who don't have a lot of time to shop, drink, and go out to eat but on shows that feature these women, that's all they do! **However**, I do like watching these kinds of shows because they are very entertaining.
>
> I think there are a few things that reality TV producers could do to make shows more "real." **First**, they could film ordinary people doing ordinary things, like taking care of their kids, grocery shopping, and cleaning their houses. **Second**, they could hire people who don't aspire to be actors and models. I think that most people who try out for reality TV shows are looking for a way to break into show business or promote products. **Third**, they could show the viewers "behind the scenes" footage about how the shows are filmed; I think that would be very interesting. **As a result**, we could get a look at people living their real lives, which to me, would be far more interesting.

Using Transition Words Correctly

Because transition words do not join two sentences, we have to be aware of the correct ways to use them. We have two choices:

1. We can join two logically related sentences with a semicolon (;) and show the logical relationship with a transition word:

   Many parents and educators are concerned about childhood obesity; **therefore**, some public school districts have banned the sale of sodas on school grounds.

The semicolon joins the two sentences, and the transition word *therefore* shows the logical relationship between them. Generally, we use this pattern when we are showing the logical relationship between two sentences.

2. We can separate the logically related sentences with a period and show the logical relationship with a transition word:

   Many parents and educators are concerned about childhood obesity. Besides promoting good exercise habits in children, these adults hope to encourage good nutrition at home and at school. **Therefore,** they want public school districts to ban the sale of high-calorie sodas on school grounds.

The transition word *therefore* shows the logical relationship between the first two sentences and the last sentence. Generally we use this pattern when we are showing the logical relationship between two idea units.

On the following page, you'll see a chart listing the transition words used most often. You can refer to this chart as you complete the exercises in this unit.

Showing Logical Relationships with Transition Words

Logical Relationship	Transition Words
Addition	also, moreover in addition furthermore besides
Cause/Effect	therefore thus as a result hence consequently
Comparison	similarly likewise
Contrast	however nevertheless nonetheless on the other hand on the contrary
Alternative	instead, rather on the other hand
Condition	otherwise
Time	then next afterwards subsequently first, second, third . . . finally meanwhile in the meantime
General to Specific	for example for instance
Restatement	in other words

Exercise One Making Connections

In this exercise, read the entire passage and then decide which transition word would effectively show the logical connection between the idea units. Write the transition word you select in the blank space.

EXAMPLE: Many American public school districts have banned the sale of sodas on school grounds because they are concerned about the growing epidemic of childhood obesity. But some parents and educators claim that a ban on soda sales alone won't be effective because children will still buy sodas, or other beverages or snacks with high sugar content, off campus. ____________, they propose that schools provide students with more opportunities for exercise and more information about nutrition during school hours.

SOLUTION: The last sentence in the preceding passage expresses an effect of the opinion expressed in the previous sentence, so any transition word showing a cause/effect connection—*therefore, thus, as a result, consequently*, or *hence*—would work. *Instead* is also possible because it shows that the parents' and educators' proposal is an alternative to the school districts' ban on soda sales.

1. Whenever I buy something new, I look in my closet to see if I have any clothes that I can give away. ______________, do I really need those bell bottoms that I bought in 1978? ______________, they might come back in style. I need to make a choice as to what to keep and what to give away as I have only limited closet space.

2. Some cities are banning the sale of large soft drinks, saying that the sugar content is to blame for the rise in the obesity rate in this country. ______________, some companies are now cutting down on the amount of sugar that they put in their soft drinks so that they can still be sold in large cup sizes. ______________, they are also calling some of their products "healthy choice" to get around certain size restrictions.

3. Since many of my friends root for different baseball teams, we often battle about which team is best. Sometimes we take a vote before watching a game, and the majority gets to watch the team of their choice on television. ______________, the losers wait impatiently until the program is over, often criticizing the team playing.

4. Some people oppose stem cell research if it involves embryonic stem cells that come from fertilized eggs donated by patients in fertility clinics. These opponents believe that fertilized eggs are already human life. ______________, scientists can sidestep the controversy surrounding the use of fertilized eggs by creating embryonic stem cells through merging unfertilized eggs with other body cells, such as skin cells.

5. Once Madeline decided that she needed to lose weight, she began to make a plan because she knew that she wouldn't naturally change her junk-food or couch-potato habits. She knew that group support would help keep her on track. ______________, she enrolled in a fitness club and joined Weight Watchers.

Exercise Two Touring Museums

In the following exercise, you will show logical relationships between sentences using transition words. Decide how the two ideas are logically related; then, choose a transition word to show the logical relationship. Join the two sentences with a semicolon and the transition word.

EXAMPLE: After he finishes his college education, Robert hopes to become an art appraiser. He's majoring in art history and minoring in business.

SOLUTION: After he finishes his college education, Robert hopes to become an art appraiser; **therefore,** he's majoring in art history and minoring in business.

1. As they planned their vacation together, Melissa and Robert knew that they wanted to escape the foggy San Francisco summer and visit museums.
   They decided on a weekend trip to sunny Los Angeles.

2. After they bought plane tickets on the Internet, they flew from San Francisco to the Los Angeles Airport, rented a compact car, and drove to West LA.
   They checked into a motel and went for a swim.

3. After they swam for an hour, they decided over lunch to spend one day visiting museums. They wanted to spend one day at the beach and another day at Universal Studios.

4. Melissa wanted to go to the Museum of Jurassic Technology to study the seed-gathering behavior of mobile home dwellers because she wanted to expand her knowledge.
   Robert wanted to go to the California Heritage Museum to see California pottery.

5. They could have spent the day arguing about where to go, but they didn't want to waste time.
   They decided to compromise.

6. They went to the Museum of Jurassic Technology in the morning and to the California Heritage Museum in the afternoon.
   They didn't have time to tour Universal Studios.

7. As Melissa toured the Museum of Jurassic Technology, she learned a lot about the behavior of seed gatherers.
   She learned that they preserve the seeds of indigenous plants.

8. While Robert walked through the California Heritage Museum, he discovered many California potters he had never heard of.
   He saw pottery from the Arts and Crafts movement.

9. When they returned to San Francisco, Melissa started planning another trip.
   Robert started visiting the local museums.

10. Since their trip was so successful, next year they're going to the Metropolitan Museum in New York.
    They might go to the Art Institute of Chicago.

Exercise Three Smooth Traveling

While it's important to know how to use transition words correctly, it's also important to know when to use them effectively to keep our writing fluent. Read the following paragraph aloud, making sure to pause when you come to a period:

> I have always enjoyed traveling. Therefore, I do it as often as I can. For example, every summer I get away, preferably to another country either in South America or in Europe. However, I don't always get a chance to leave this country. Sometimes I don't have enough money. Furthermore, I am sometimes too busy to take off a month or two to travel. Nevertheless, I usually do everything I can to get away. For example, I will work 55-hour weeks, spend nothing on myself, and go without luxuries such as a car or dining out, just to save enough money for my trips. In addition, I even try to survive on peanut butter sandwiches or baked potatoes to save money for my plane tickets.

What is the problem with this paragraph? What do you hear? ____________________

____

Here's the same paragraph, but now without the transition words.

> I have always enjoyed traveling. I do it as often as I can. Every summer I get away, preferably to another country either in South America or in Europe. I don't always get a chance to leave this country. Sometimes I don't have enough money. I am sometimes too busy to take off a month or two to travel. I usually do everything I can to get away. I work 55-hour weeks, spend nothing on myself, and go without luxuries such as a car or dining out, just to save enough money for my trips. I even try to survive on peanut butter sandwiches or baked potatoes to save money for my plane tickets.

What is the problem with this paragraph? What do you hear now? ________________

____

In this exercise, rewrite the above paragraph, using coordinators and subordinators to join logically-related sentences. Is there a place where a transition word would be effective? If you need more space, you can continue writing on the back of this page.

SUMMARY: Transition words can be effective ways to show logical connections between ideas—to make transitions clear for readers. But it's important to use them effectively and correctly, to make sure that they don't take over your writing. Aim to use transition words to show logical relationships between sets of ideas, and use a variety of coordinators and subordinators to show logical connections between sentences or parts of sentences.

Exercise Four You Be the Author

My dog loves to roll around in the mud, and since I live in the rainy Northwest, we always have a lot of mud puddles in our yard. ____________, he has to be bathed at least twice a week or more if the weather is particularly bad. It takes a lot of work to get him ready for the bath. ____________, I take off his collar, which usually indicates to him that something he won't like is about to happen. ____________, I pick him up and put him in the bathtub, making sure that I have a washcloth handy so that I can get him wet quickly and get rid of all of the dirt on his coat. ____________, I wash him down, hoping he won't shake the water off and get me soaked. ____________, after that process, I rub him down with a dry towel and hope that he doesn't have to go out any time soon.

Unit Nine

Joining Parallel Structures

The coordinators *and*, *or*, and *but* can join parts of sentences; the sentence parts are called parallel because they are similar grammatical structures that express similar ideas. The parallel structures in the sentences below are underlined:

> Shauna and Lisa watch movies every weekend.
> Shauna laughs or cries all during the films.
> Lisa eats popcorn constantly but quietly.

In the following exercise, you will be joining sets of sentences like the ones given in following example. (Notice the crossed-out words; when you join parallel structures, you can be more concise because you avoid repeating words.) The joining word *and*, *or*, or *but* is given in brackets to tell you which word to use.

EXAMPLE: Latisha ate a burrito.
~~Latisha ate~~ a taco. *[and]*

SOLUTION: Latisha ate a burrito and a taco.

EXAMPLE: Rudy started the car.
~~Rudy~~ backed out of the driveway. *[and]*

SOLUTION: Rudy started the car and backed out of the driveway.

Exercise One The Decision

1. Sonia was planning to move into the dorms.
   Sonia was planning to move into an apartment with a friend. *[or]*

2. She listed the benefits of each place.
   She listed the drawbacks of each place. *[and]*

3. The apartment was close to campus.
   The apartment was close to the mall. *[and]*

4. The dorm fee was more expensive.
   It included room and board. *[but]*

5. She could have her own room in the apartment.
   She would have to share a dorm room with another student. *[but]*

6. Sonia knew her friend was studious and responsible.
   Sonia didn't know what her dorm roommate would be like. *[but]*

7. Sonia discussed her options with her parents.
   Sonia discussed her options with her friends. *[and]*

8. Her parents thought she should wait a year before moving out.
   Her friends agreed. *[and]*

9. Sonia chose to reject her parents' advice.
   Sonia chose to reject her friends' advice. *[and]*

10. She decided to enroll in Clown College.
    She decided to at least join the local circus. *[or]*

Joining Three or More Parallel Ideas

The coordinators *and*, *or*, and *but* can also join three or more elements in a sentence; all of the elements should have similar grammatical structures.

EXAMPLE: Shauna, her boyfriend, and Lisa watch movies every weekend.
Latisha ate a burrito, a taco, and a banana split.
Rudy started the car, backed out of the driveway, and crashed into the potted plant.

Often a series of parallel structures has descriptive modifiers:

Yesterday I finished my homework,
took my sister to the dentist,
cooked dinner,
and went to bed at midnight.

The important thing is that the parallel parts—the verbs *finished*, *took*, *cooked*, and *went*—all have the same grammatical structure and can follow the sentence subject—*I*.

Exercise Two Sleepaway Camp

Combine the following sets of sentences to create one sentence that contains a parallel series of two, three, or four parts. The coordinators are given in brackets.

EXAMPLE: Patrick went to sleepaway camp.
His brother Alex went to sleepaway camp. *[and]*
His best friend Luke went to sleepaway camp.

SOLUTION: Patrick, his brother Alex, *and* his best friend Luke went to sleepaway camp.

1. They wanted to live in the woods.
They wanted to learn how to camp outdoors. *[and]*
They wanted to become independent.

2. Patrick thought he could become a counselor in a few years. *[or]*
Patrick thought he could become a bunk leader. *[but]*
Patrick was lazy.

3. Alex wanted to learn how to pitch a tent. *[and]*
Alex wanted to meet a lot of people. *[but]*
Alex kept to himself.

4. Luke wanted experience as a trail guide. *[and]*
Luke wanted opportunities to lead hikes. *[and]*
Luke wanted to rock climb.

5. Luke became an excellent hike leader.
   Luke was promoted to counselor in training. *[and]*
   Luke began to give orders to Patrick and Alex.

6. Patrick soon realized that he would never become a counselor. *[or]*
   Patrick realized that he would never become a bunk leader. *[and]*
   He grew tired of taking orders.

7. Alex met a lot of people. *[and]*
   Morton made a lot of friends. *[but]*
   He didn't have any other interests at camp.

8. Patrick decided to go home. *[and]*
   Alex decided to go home. *[but]*
   They disagreed over when to leave.

9. Patrick wanted Alex to call their mother.
   Patrick wanted Alex to tell her that they were homesick. *[and]*

10. Luke discovered their plot. *[and]*
    Luke threatened to tell the head counselor. *[or]*
    Luke threatened to tell the boys' mother that they were lazy. *[but]*
    Patrick promised to continue taking orders. *[and]*
    Alex lead everyone in a singalong.

Exercise Three You Be the Co-Author

In this exercise, you will create parallel structures matching the underlined words to complete the sentences. Remember to join the parallel structures with *and*, *but*, or *or* before the last item in the list of parallel structures. Try to use all three of the coordinators that join parallel structures.

EXAMPLE: My favorite foods are burritos, ________________________________

____

SOLUTION: My favorite foods are burritos, pasta, broccoli, peaches, and chocolate cake

1. To have a happy childhood, children should have a safe home, ____________________

____

2. Once I graduate from college, I'll go to graduate school, ____________________

____

3. People can protect the environment by recycling, ____________________

____

4. I sometimes envy students who are good at statistics, ____________________

____

5. I'd like to travel to Mexico, ____________________

____

6. I wish the U.S. government would provide better health care, ____________________

____

7. My closest friend is reliable, ____________________

____

8. Whenever I'm looking for a job, I <u>search</u> the want-ads, ______________________________

____

9. I spent the weekend <u>cleaning</u> my kitchen, ______________________________

____

10. <u>Watching</u> movies, ____

____

are my favorite things to do.

In the following exercise, you will use coordinators, subordinators, and parallel structures to create one sentence from each set of sentences. The logical relationships, and suggestions for using coordinators or subordinators to express the relationships, are given in brackets. You will have to discover which parts of sentences can be joined with *and*, *or*, or *but* to form parallel structures. Always plan your solution and read your combined sentences aloud.

EXAMPLE: People have long argued about whether genes determine our personalities the most.
People have long argued about whether the environment determines our personalities the most.
[coordinator—contrast] Now many scientists believe that nature and nurture work together.

SOLUTION: People have long argued about whether genes or the environment determines our personalities the most, but now many scientists believe that nature and nurture work together.

1. Scientists now believe that genes determine only the brain's main circuits of neurons.
Scientists now believe that the environment shapes the trillions of connections between neurons.

2. *[subordinator—time]* Babies are born.
Their brains have trillions of neurons.
[coordinator—contrast] Only some of these neurons are functional.

3. Some of the neurons have already formed circuits that regulate breathing.
The circuits regulate heartbeat.
The circuits regulate body temperature.
The circuits regulate reflexes.

4. Other neurons have not formed circuits.
[subordinator or coordinator—cause] These neurons become functional only when they respond to outside stimuli.

5. *[subordinator—condition or time]* The neurons are stimulated.
   They are integrated into the circuitry of the brain.
   [subordinator or coordinator—cause] They connect to other neurons.

6. *[subordinator—condition]* The neurons are not stimulated.
   The neurons may wither.
   The neurons may die.

7. Childhood experiences stimulate neurons.
   Childhood experiences determine whether a child will be confident.
   Childhood experiences determine whether a child will be fearful.

8. Experiments with rats show new evidence that the neurons can be stimulated with play.
   Experiments are with monkeys.
   Experiments are with human babies.
   The neurons can be stimulated with purposeful training.

9. Scientists have found that music helps develop children's brain circuits.
   [coordinator—effect] Parents should sing songs with their children.
   Parents should play structured, melodic music.
   Parents should give their children music lessons.
   [subordinator—condition] Their children show musical aptitude.
   Their children show musical interest.

10. *[subordinator—time]* Children listen to classical music.
 They exercise neurons.
 They strengthen circuits for mathematics.
 [subordinator—cause] The brain circuits for math are close to the circuits for music.

11. Scientists have found that talking to children helps develop children's brain circuits for language.
 [coordinator—effect] Parents should talk to their children a lot.

12. Parents can also influence their children's circuits for emotions.
 [subordinator—condition] The parents recognize their children's emotions.
 The parents return their children's emotions.

13. *[subordinator—condition or time]* A parent approves of his or her child's happiness.
 The child's circuits for happy emotions are reinforced.

14. *[subordinator—condition or time]* A parent disapproves of his or her child's happiness.
 The circuits are confused.
 The circuits will not strengthen.

15. *[subordinator—condition or time]* A parent hugs an upset child.
 The child learns to calm himself or herself down.

16. *[subordinator—condition or time]* A parent yells at an upset child.
The child doesn't learn to calm himself or herself down.
[subordinator or coordinator—cause] The parent's response does not stimulate the circuits for calming down.

17. But the parent's actions have to be repeated over time.
[subordinator or coordinator—cause] One mistake will not scar a child for life.

18. *[subordinator—cause]* Environmental influences begin early in life.
People often confuse them with genetic causes.
[coordinator—contrast] Actually, the environmental stimuli are crucial for a child's development.

Unit Ten

Modifying Nouns with Adjectives

In conversation and in writing, we often use descriptive words to add meaning to nouns—to modify them. Nouns are words that name persons, places, or things. A sentence subject is usually a noun:

The mayor spoke.

But all nouns do not act as sentence subjects; one sentence can have several nouns with different functions in the sentence:

The mayor spoke to the reporters about his plans.

In this unit, you will practice modifying nouns to create concise, detailed sentences. In the following exercises, you will be given both the nouns and the modifiers. You will first see a base sentence with its nouns underlined:

The doctor spoke to the patient.

Then you will see one or more sentences repeating those underlined nouns and providing you with new information to use to modify the nouns in the base sentence. Be sure you find all the new information; one way to do so is to cross out any repeated words and any forms of the verb *be* in the sentences containing modifiers.

EXAMPLE: The doctor spoke to the patient.
~~The doctor was~~ sympathetic.
~~The patient was~~ overweight.

Then add the adjective modifiers to the basic sentence:

SOLUTION: The *sympathetic* doctor spoke to the *overweight* patient.

In each set of sentences, your goal is to end up with one sentence. Always read your combined sentences aloud to see if they sound correct to you. These exercises will help you write more detailed, professional sentences.

NOTE: When you add a modifier before a noun, you sometimes have to change the article in the base sentence from a to an or an to a because the modifier you add begins with a different letter than the noun does. Use a before words beginning with consonant sounds, and an before words beginning with vowel sounds.

EXAMPLES:	a dog	a horse	a university
	an apple	an hour	an umbrella

Exercise One Never Too Young

1. Doctors are concerned about their patients.
   The doctors are concerned.
   Their patients are overweight.

2. They have warned them to modify their diets for years.
   The diets are daily.
   The years are many.

3. But their patients continue to eat too much food.
   The patients are stubborn.
   The patients are busy.
   The food is fatty.
   The food is not nutritious.

4. Amounts of food can cause levels that, in turn, can cause heart disease.
   The amounts are large.
   The food is high-fat.*
   The levels are high.
   The levels are cholesterol.

*Hyphenated adjectives such as *high-fat*, *health-conscious*, or *middle-aged* act like one-word modifiers and go before the nouns they modify:

Jack has been following a low-cholestetol diet for years.

5. Of course, not all people are at risk.
   The people are healthy.
   The risk is high.

6. In particular, doctors believe that people who have a history of coronary disease should be concerned.
   The doctors are conscientious.
   The people are middle-aged.
   The history is family.
   The disease is heart-related.

7. The thing for all people to do is cut down on food.
   The people are health-conscious.
   The food is fatty.
   The food is highly processed.

8. People can start now to protect their health by eating more chicken, fish, fruit and vegetables, and dairy products.
   The people are younger.
   The chicken is skinless.
   The fish is broiled or baked.
   The fruit and vegetables are fresh.
   The dairy products are low-fat.

Verb Forms as Adjectives

In the previous exercise, each modifier you added was a single adjective that you placed in front of the noun it modified. But verb forms can also act like adjectives and modify nouns:

The movie is frightening the child.	The child is frightened (by the movie).
→ the *frightening* movie	→the *frightened* child

The *-ing* forms (present participles) and the *-ed* forms of verbs (past participles) can often modify nouns. Notice that when *frightening* and *frightened* are parts of verbs in sentences, they follow forms of the verb *be*: *am, is, are, was, were, has been, have been, and had been*. But when these *-ing* and *-ed* ending verb forms modify nouns, they are not parts of verbs any longer; that is, they do not show the time, or tense, of sentences. The following are common verb form modifiers:

***-ing* Form**	***-ed* Form**
the *interesting* novel	the *interested* reader
the *terrifying* train ride	the *terrified* passengers
the *annoying* salesclerk	the *annoyed* shoppers

If the verb form modifier is a single word, you can place it before the noun it modifies:

EXAMPLE: The farmer ran from the bull.
The farmer was *frightened*.
The bull was *charging*.

SOLUTION: The *frightened* farmer ran from the *charging* bull.

Often, though, we modify nouns with modifiers that have more than one word:

***-ing* Form**	***-ed* Form**
the man *buying the book at Green Apple*	the book *bought at Green Apple*
the woman *building the bridge*	the bridge *built by the woman*

When the modifier is more than one word, it comes after the word it modifies.

Exercise Two Double Dutch

In this exercise, the nouns to be modified are underlined. Add the common adjectives and the verb form modifiers before or after the nouns they modify. One-word modifiers should come before the nouns they modify, and modifiers of more than one word should come after the nouns they modify.

EXAMPLE: Many adults remember Double Dutch as a game.
The adults are American.
~~The adults are~~ reminiscing about their childhoods.
~~The game was~~ played on their neighborhood streets.

SOLUTION: Many *American* adults *reminiscing about their childhoods* remember Double Dutch as a game *played on their neighborhood streets.*

1. Double Dutch is a sport.
   The sport is demanding.
   The sport is competitive.
   The sport is played by jumpers skipping within two spinning jump ropes.

2. Every year, thousands of teenagers compete to be on teams.
   The teenagers are talented.
   The teenagers are living all over the world.
   The teams are representing their schools and clubs.

3. A form has become popular.
   The form is new.
   The form is called fusion.
   The form is combining rope jumping and dancing.

4. Teams perform routines in competitions.
   The teams are youthful.
   The routines are sophisticated.
   The routines are accompanied by rhymes, rhythm and blues, or rap.
   The competitions are international.

5. The <u>jumpers</u> execute <u>steps</u>.
   The jumpers are agile.
   The steps are including "The Scissor Jump" and "The Caterpillar."

6. Some <u>teams</u> jump to <u>music</u> and <u>rap</u>.
   The teams are award-winning.
   The teams are Japanese.
   The music is traditional.
   The rap is hardcore.

7. The jumpers sense the ropes' <u>beat</u>.
   The beat is set by the rope turners.

8. Double Dutch probably originated with <u>rope-makers</u>.
   The rope-makers were Phoenician, Egyptian, and Chinese.
   The rope-makers were spinning rope from hemp.

9. The <u>rope-makers</u> made a <u>game</u> from their <u>work</u>.
   The rope-makers were resourceful.
   The game was leisure-time.
   Their work was demanding.

10. Many people are surprised that this <u>game</u> is called Double Dutch.
    The game is urban.
    The game is loved by children of all ages.

Exercise Three Hairdos—The Assyrians and Us

In the following exercise, you will continue adding adjectives and verb form modifiers to the base sentences, but this time the nouns to be modified aren't underlined for you. In the sentences containing modifiers, cross out repeated words and forms of the verb *be—am*, *is*, *are*, *was*, and *were*.

EXAMPLE: In the ancient world, the Assyrians were the hair stylists.
~~The Assyrians were~~ living in Iraq.
~~The hair stylists were the~~ first.
~~The hair stylists were~~ real.

SOLUTION: In the ancient world, the Assyrians *living in Iraq* were the *first real* hair stylists.

1. The Assyrians cut hair in layers, so a man's head was like a pyramid.
The layers were graduated.
The man was fashionable.
The pyramid was Egyptian.

2. Hair was arranged in curls and ringlets.
The curls were cascading.
The ringlets were tumbling over the shoulders.

3. Men grew beards.
The beards were neatly clipped.
The beards were beginning at the jaw.
The beards were layered in ruffles over the chest.

4. Women also wore beards.
   Women were high-ranking.
   The beards were stylized.
   The beards were fake.
   The beards were designed to make the women appear like powerful men.

5. Kings, warriors, and noblewomen had their hair curled with a bar.
   Their hair was abundant.
   Their hair was flowing.
   The bar was fire-heated.
   The bar was iron.

6. Now people have hair styles or bald heads.
   The people are young.
   The hair styles are sculpted.
   The heads are partially shaven.
   The bald heads are decorated with letters or designs.

7. But women don't wear beards.
   The women are modern.
   The beards are designed to give them equal status to men.

Exercise Four You Be the Author

In this exercise, you will create complete sentences containing the three nouns you are given and the adjective modifiers that you invent. Be sure to use both modifiers that come before nouns and modifiers that come after nouns.

EXAMPLE: students bus bus stop

SOLUTION: The *exhausted* students *carrying backpacks* waited for the *late* bus at the *crowded* bus stop

1.	rain	trees	leaves
2.	guitarist	music	heavy metal
3.	doctor	note	employer
4.	dancer	stage	audience
5.	coffee	café	night
6.	fish	lake	rod
7.	sister	dress	party
8.	cousin	junk	car
9.	trainer	exercise	client
10.	chef	kitchen	tomatoes

Unit Eleven

Modifying Nouns with Prepositional Phrases

Prepositional phrases, groups of words beginning with prepositions such as *in*, *on*, *near*, *of*, *with*, *about*, *at*, *to*, *for*, and *from*, can also modify nouns. Prepositional phrases have many purposes.

They often tell place:

We bought a house *in the country.*
The keys *on the desk* are mine.
She owns the cafe *near the railroad station*.

But they often give other information as well:

Everyone knows the dangers *of smoking*.
I bought a car *with a sunroof*.
She wrote a novel *about evil politicians*.

In this unit, you will use prepositional phrases to modify nouns. Like other modifiers of more than one word that you studied in Unit Nine, prepositional phrases come after the nouns they modify:

EXAMPLE: The dance club admits everyone.
~~The dance club is~~ for teenagers.
~~Everyone is~~ between 18 and 21.

SOLUTION: The dance club *for teenagers* admits everyone *between 18 and 21.*

Just as you did in the exercises on adjective modifiers in the previous unit, try crossing out repeated words and forms of the verb *be* in the sentences containing the prepositional phrases; then, place the prepositional phrases after the nouns they modify in the base sentence.

Exercise One Rescue Pets

In this exercise, the nouns you should modify are underlined. Create one sentence from each set of sentences, placing the prepositional phrases after the nouns they modify. As you did in the adjective modifier unit, cross out repeated words and forms of *be* in the sentences containing prepositional phrases.

EXAMPLE: Brian rarely leaves his home for trips.
~~His home is~~ in the city.
~~The trips are~~ in the wild.

SOLUTION: Brian rarely leaves his home *in the city* for trips *in the wild*

EXAMPLE: Many people visit animal shelters to adopt pets.
~~The animal shelters are~~ in adjacent towns.
~~The pets are~~ of varying ages.

SOLUTION: Many people visit animal shelters *in adjacent towns* to adopt pets *of varying ages*.

1. My friend persuaded me to join her on a shelter visit.
My friend is in a rescue organization.
The shelter was in the country.

2. We rented a van, set out for the shelter, and got caught in traffic.
The shelter was by a highway.
The traffic was from San Francisco.

3. When we finally arrived, we saw a lot of dogs.
We arrived at ten.
The dogs were in a large gated area.

4. I saw a beautiful retriever puppy.
The puppy was under a blanket.
The puppy was without a name tag.

5. We took the puppy out of the cage.
We took the puppy for a walk.
We walked by a stream.

6. When it was time to leave, I went back and saw the puppy.
   The puppy was in the shelter's director's arms.
   The puppy was under a blanket.

7. After a few minutes of thought, I decided to take the puppy to my home.
   The thought was conflicted.
   My home is in the suburbs.
   My home is next to a big park.

8. I left my apartment the next morning and took the puppy to the park.
   I left my apartment at ten.
   I took the puppy to the park next to the mall.

9. While the puppy played, I rested.
   The puppy played with other dogs.
   I rested in the grass.
   I rested by a group of dog owners.

10. I named the dog Alice after Alice in Wonderland.
    Alice in Wonderland is by Lewis Carroll.

Exercise Two Global Warming

In this exercise, you will again practice using prepositional phrases to modify the underlined nouns. Plan your solutions by crossing out repeated nouns and forms of the verb *be* in the sentences containing prepositional phrase modifiers.

EXAMPLE: A radical shift is under way and human dependence is at least partly to blame.
~~The shift is~~ in the Earth's climate.
~~The dependence is~~ on fossil fuels.

SOLUTION:: A radical shift *in the Earth's climate* is under way, and human dependence *on fossil fuels* is at least partly to blame.

1. Heat enters the atmosphere and warms the surface.
The heat is from the Sun.
The surface is of the Earth.

2. Carbon dioxide and other greenhouse gases trap the heat, causing global warming—rising temperatures and rising levels.
The temperatures are in regions.
The regions are throughout the world.
The rising levels are of oceans.

3. The burning is the main source that produces greenhouses gases.
The burning is of fossil fuels.
The source is of human-caused carbon dioxide.

4. Currently, emissions are expected to double in the next 100 years unless people take action.
The emissions are of greenhouse gases such as carbon dioxide, methane, and nitrous oxides.
The people are throughout the world.

5. Already there are signs.
   The signs are of far-reaching ecological effects.

6. Glaciers, the Greenland ice cap, and the ice shelves are shrinking.
   The glaciers are in the Swiss Alps.
   The ice shelves are in Antarctica.

7. We are also witnessing the growth.
   The growth is of El Niños.
   The growth is in strength and frequency.

8. Most scientists think that a rapid change will produce more frequent and severe droughts and floods, widening epidemics, and greater loss.
   The change is in the Earth's climate.
   The epidemics are of infectious diseases.
   The loss is of biological diversity.

9. Scientists are studying alternate forms, including fuels made from fermented grasses, solar panels, and vast networks.
   The forms are of energy.
   The panels are on rooftops.
   The networks are of wind turbines, hydroelectric dams, and big heat exchangers.

10. Fortunately, there is no shortage.
    The shortage is of solar energy, the primary alternative.
    The alternative is to fossil fuels.

Nessie

Review Exercise 3

In the following review exercises, you will practice using the modifiers from Units Ten and Eleven—adjective and verb form modifiers and prepositional phrases. This time the nouns to be modified are not underlined. Continue crossing out repeated words and forms of the verb *be*.

EXAMPLE: Since the 6th century A.D., people have seen a beast.
~~The people are~~ in the Scottish Highlands.
~~The beast is~~ strange.
~~The beast is~~ in a lake.
~~The lake is~~ deep.
~~The lake is~~ dark.
~~The lake is~~ called Loch Ness.

SOLUTION: Since the 6th century A.D., people *in the Scottish Highlands* have seen a *strange* beast *in a deep, dark lake called Loch Ness.*

1. In the 20th century, scientists have tried to substantiate tales.
The tales are outlandish.
The tales are of the monster.
The monster is now named the Loch Ness Monster, or Nessie.

2. Witnesses report that the monster is a creature.
The monster is 20-feet long.*
The creature is long-necked.
The creature is full-bodied.
The creature is with eyes.
The eyes are large.
The eyes are oval-shaped.
The eyes are on top of a head.
The head is small.
The head is snakelike.

3. Many stories come from residents and observers.
The stories are about the monster.
The residents are respected in the community.
The observers are visiting from Europe and abroad.

*When a modifier showing size is placed before a noun, the word denoting size is singular; we say a 20-foot-long monster, 60-pound girl, or 20-yard line.

4. Some of the stories may be legends.
   The stories are told by residents.
   The residents are along Loch Ness' shores.
   The legends are old.
   The legends are passed down from grandparents to children.
   The children are gathered around firesides.

5. Some people believe the tales are plots to attract tourists.
   The plots are created by hotel owners and shopkeepers.
   The tourists are gullible.
   The tourists are hoping to spend money.

6. Tourists can buy models or plaques.
   The models are miniature.
   The models are of the monster.
   The plaques are commemorative.
   The plaques are imprinted with Nessie's picture.

7. Some biologists believe the monster is really an otter, a deer, or a log.
   The otter is large.
   The otter is playing in the water.
   The deer is swimming across the lake.
   The log is half-submerged.
   The log is decaying.

8. Other scientists believe Nessie could be a descendant of reptiles.
The reptiles were giant.
The reptiles were ocean-dwelling.
The reptiles were trapped in lakes.
The lakes were inland.
The lakes were cut off from the ocean by glaciers.

9. Particles make the lake difficult to explore.
The particles are coffee-colored.
The particles are peat.
The particles are floating in the water.
The lake is deep.
The lake is steep-sided.

10. Teams have investigated Loch Ness with searchlights, radar, cameras, submarines, and equipment.
The teams are of scientists.
The radar is underwater.
The cameras are underwater.
The submarines are manned.
The equipment is recording.
The equipment is packed inside oil drums.
The oil drums are watertight.

11. In the 1970s, scientists accepted proof.
    The scientists are renowned.
    The scientists are from all over the world.
    The proof is of Nessie's existence.
    The proof is in the form of photographs.
    The photographs are showing features.
    The features are facial.
    The features are of an object.
    The object is living.

12. But scientists still don't know what the object is.
    The object is unidentified.
    The object is swimming.

Sutro Baths Nostalgia

Review Exercise 4

With each set of sentences, create one sentence using simple adjectives, verb form adjectives, and prepositional phrases to modify nouns. Plan your solution by crossing out repeated nouns and forms of the verb *be* in the sentences containing the modifiers. Be sure to read your sentences aloud after you finish each one.

EXAMPLE

Sutro Baths was a palace.
~~Sutro Baths was~~ at the end.
~~The end is~~ northern.
~~The end is~~ of Ocean Beach.
~~Ocean Beach is~~ in San Francisco.
~~The palace was~~ huge.
~~The palace was~~ of swimming pools.
~~The pools were~~ for the whole family.

SOLUTION: Sutro Baths, *at the northern end of Ocean Beach in San Francisco,* was a *huge* palace *of swimming pools for the whole family.*

1. The swimming pools were the baths in an era.
The swimming pools were completed in 1894.
The baths were the largest.
The baths were enclosed.
The baths were saltwater.
The baths were in the world.
The era was of many pools.
The pools were indoor.
The pools were saltwater.

2. In 1894, more than 20,000 people attended the inauguration.
The people were pleasure-loving.
The inauguration was featuring a concert and races.
The concert was orchestral.
The races were by swimmers.
The swimmers were competitive.

3. Sutro Baths also had a museum, a gallery, and a gymnasium.
   The museum was exhibiting collections.
   The collections were various.
   The collections were in display cases.
   The gallery was of photographs.
   The gymnasium was filled with trapezes and rings.

4. Visitors descended a staircase to pools.
   The staircase was wide.
   The staircase was bordered with trees.
   The trees were palm, pomegranate, and magnolia.
   The pomegranate trees were flowering.
   The magnolia trees were fragrant.
   The pools were glass-enclosed.
   The pools were facing the ocean.

5. Visitors could choose between a plunge and other pools.
   The plunge was large.
   The plunge was L-shaped.
   The plunge was unheated.
   The other pools were of temperatures.
   The temperatures were varied.
   The other pools were including one bath.
   The bath was freshwater.

6. Water came from basins and a spring.
   The water was for the pools.
   The basins were constructed in the cliffs.
   The cliffs were fronting the ocean.
   The spring was ever-flowing.
   The spring was freshwater.

7. Around the pools were tiers and balconies.
   The tiers were of seats.
   The seats were for 5,000 people.
   The balconies were for 15,000 more spectators.
   The spectators were wandering.

8. Each tier had corridors.
   The corridors were decorated with plants, fountains, and creatures.
   The plants were tropical.
   The creatures were stuffed.
   The creatures were in life-like poses.

9. By 1952, Sutro Baths had undergone changes.
   The changes were many.
   The changes were including the additions and the closing.
   The additions were of an ice-skating rink and a beach.
   The beach was interior.
   The beach was tropical.
   The closing was of the pools.
   The pools were deteriorating.

10. But Sutro Baths closed in 1952 and the remains later burned to the ground.
    Sutro Baths were costly.
    The remains were of the building.

11. Now San Franciscans swim in pools.
    The pools are crowded.
    The pools are chlorinated.
    The pools are divided into lanes.
    The lanes are for lap swimmers.

Review Exercises 5 and 6 make use of all of the structures you have learned in previous lessons: adjective modifiers, prepositional phrase modifiers, coordinators, subordinators, and parallel structures.

NOTE: You should use coordinators and subordinators only where you see brackets that tell you which logical relationship to show.

EXAMPLE: [*subordinator—contrast*] The child is hungry.
The child is stubborn.
The child refuses to eat.

SOLUTION: Although the stubborn child is hungry, he refuses to eat.

For each set of sentences, create one sentence, joining related ideas with coordinators, subordinators, and parallel structures and modifying nouns with adjectives and prepositional phrases.

EXAMPLE: Plastics have been around for over a century.
[*coordinator—effect*] We now take them for granted.

SOLUTION: Plastics have been around for over a century, so we now take them for granted.

1. Our lifestyle depends heavily on plastics.
   Our lifestyle is modern.
   Our lifestyle is convenient.
   [subordinator or coordinator—cause] They are lightweight, resistant to corrosion, and durable.

2. ***[subordinator—condition]*** We look around.
   We can see that this marvel has practically invaded our society.
   The marvel is synthetic.

3. Pans, windows, and bumpers are a few items that have made our lives easier.
   The pans are nonstick.
   The pans are Teflon-coated.
   The windows are shatterproof.
   The windows are plastic.
   The bumpers are nonrusting.
   The bumpers are plastic.
   The bumpers are on cars.
   [coordinator—contrast] Plastics have also become a menace.
   The menace is to our environment.

4. ***[subordinator—cause]*** Plastic does not decompose.
   Wastes accumulate in piles.
   The piles are enormous.
   The piles are unsanitary.
   The piles are in city dumps.

5. ***[subordinator—cause]*** Ocean dumping used to be legal.
   Our oceans are now filled with plastics.
   The plastics are dangerous.

6. Every year, trash kills or maims thousands.
   The trash is floating.
   The trash is plastic.
   The thousands are of sea creatures.

7. As many as 40,000 seals die from starvation or strangulation each year.
   [subordinator—time] They become entangled in netting and packing straps.
   The netting and packing straps are plastic.

8. Many sea creatures eat bags and fishing lines that resemble jellyfish or plankton.
   The bags and lines are plastic.
   [coordinator—effect] They die from stomach blockage or bleeding.
   The bleeding is internal.

9. The effects are devastating.
   The effects are of plastics disposal.
   [coordinator—contrast] Some solutions may be on the horizon.

10. Some scientists can make products.
    The products are biodegradable.
    The products are plastic.
    The products are from a mixture.
    The mixture is of cornstarch and plastic.
    [subordinator—contrast] Scientists worry that the dust could be harmful to breathe.
    The dust is fine.
    The dust is of plastic.
    The plastic is decomposing.

11. Other scientists think wastes could be burned for fuel.
    The wastes are plastic.
    [subordinator or coordinator—cause] Most plastic is made from petroleum.

12. The idea seems good.
    The idea is of burning plastic for fuel.
    [subordinator—condition] Technology for burning can be developed.
    The burning is safe.
    The burning is of plastic.

13. Meanwhile, the whales, seals, and turtles must wait for a generation to work out a solution.
    The generation is new.
    The generation is of scientists.
    The scientists are knowledgeable.
    The scientists are concerned.
    The solution is to our plastic waste problem.

Review Exercise 6

In the following exercise, you will not be given any cues signaling when to use joining words, so this exercise may seem more challenging than previous review exercises. And although these exercises call for structures you have already worked with in this book, you may come up with alternative ways to combine some of these more open sentence sets.

EXAMPLE: Perhaps you have a pen or a bracelet.
The pen is lucky.
The pen is for writing "A" essays.
The bracelet is favorite.
The bracelet is of lucky charms.
You keep your superstitions secret.

SOLUTION: Perhaps you have a lucky pen for writing "A" essays or a favorite bracelet of lucky charms, but you keep your superstitions secret.

1. You may be embarrassed to admit to your superstitions.
People have had superstitions.
The people are from all cultures and times.
The superstitions are about events and objects.
The events are natural.

2a. The rabbit's foot was a symbol.
The symbol was of good luck.
The symbol was for Celtic tribes.
The Celtic tribes were in Western Europe around 600 b.c.
Celtic tribes believed the rabbit was in contact with forces.
The rabbit was burrowing.
The forces were mysterious.
The forces were from the underground.

2b. The rabbit bears young quite frequently.
The Celtic people considered the rabbit a symbol.
The symbol was powerful.
The symbol was of fertility.

2c. They came to treasure the rabbit's foot.
They believed it could promote fertility.
The fertility was in women.

3a. Adults knock on wood.
The adults are boasting.
They are participating in a 4,000-year-old ritual.
The ritual is Native American Indian.

3b. The Native American Indians believed that boasting could bring bad luck.
The boasting was about a future accomplishment.
They sought to appease the gods by knocking on an oak tree.

4a. Many of us know about the tradition.
The tradition is of breaking a wishbone.
We may not know its origins.

4b. The Etruscans believed that hens and roosters were prophets.
The Etruscans were ancient.
The Etruscans were in Italy.
The hens were squawking before laying an egg.
The roosters were crowing to "foretell" a new day.

4c. Originally, the Etruscans made wishes by stroking the bones.
The bones were unbroken.
The bones were dried.
The bones were clavicle.
The bones were of roosters and hens.

4d. Later, the practice changed.
The practice was of stroking the clavicle.
The reason is not especially mysterious.
The reason is for this change.

4e. Eventually, the custom came about.
The custom was of two people.
The people were tugging at the wishbone to get the larger half.
Too many people wanted to make wishes on too few wishbones.

4f. This superstition survives today in our expression "to get a lucky break."
The superstition is of the wishbone.

5a. We all have heard that walking brings bad luck.
The walking is under a ladder.
Most are unaware that this superstition goes back to about 3000 B.C. in Egypt.

5b. The triangle represented a trinity.
The triangle was created when a ladder was leaned against a wall.
The trinity was sacred.
The trinity was of gods.

5c. People walked under a ladder.
They were violating space.
The space was sacred.

6a. A new baby is born.
The parents sometimes tell their children that the stork delivered the baby down the chimney.
This explanation is confusing today.

6b. The Scandinavians originated the story.
The Scandinavians were ancient.
The story is of the stork.
The Scandinavians admired the birds.
The birds are long-lived.
The birds are monogamous.

6c. The Scandinavians noticed that storks lavished attention on their parents.
The storks were adult.
The storks were nesting in chimney tops.
Their parents were elderly.

6d. The stork, therefore, became a symbol.
The symbol is of a life.
The life is long.
The life is happy.
The life is domestic.

7. Our society relies on explanations.
Our society is "civilized."
The explanations are scientific.
Many people still count on superstitions.
The superstitions are passed down from earlier generations.
Many even create their own superstitious beliefs.

Unit Twelve

Modifying Nouns with Appositives

Among the words that can modify nouns are nouns themselves. For instance, we sometimes use noun modifiers next to (before or after) the nouns they describe.

The cab driver opened the door for his passenger, a tall *woman* in a strapless red dress.

Woman is a noun that makes it clear to the reader who the passenger is; the word *woman* plus the modifiers *tall* and *in a strapless red dress* rename *passenger* in a specific way. We call the underlined descriptive phrase an appositive, which is a word or phrase containing a noun that renames the noun it modifies.

More examples:

My best friend, a cat with a loud purr, always knows how to cheer me up.

She went to see Humphrey Bogart in a romantic movie, the fifth one she'd seen in a week.

Marvin, a straight A student in chemistry, ignited his lab partner's hair with the bunson burner, a device Marvin should never have touched.

Punctuation with Appositives

Set off single modifying phrases with commas:

Carlos met his girlfriend at the health club, the local hangout.

If the appositive comes in the middle of a sentence, enclose it in commas:

Carlos met his girlfriend, a disc jockey, at the health club.

Set off a series of appositives with dashes:

Carlos and his girlfriend enjoy similar things—cartoons, Diet Coke, spandex leotards, and mirrors.
Their friends—sun-tanned gods and goddesses, the state's best aerobic instructor, and the local DJ—like to get together to party.

Or use a colon to set off a list of appositives at the end of a sentence:

> Bart wrote the following items on his shopping list: <u>Frostie Fritters Cereal, strawberry milk, hot dogs, canned dog food, and paper towels.</u>

Exercise One Online Dating

Combine the sentence sets by eliminating, in the second sentence, the noun that repeats the noun in the first sentence. Also eliminate any forms of the verb *be* so that you reduce the second sentence to an appositive that modifies the underlined noun in the first sentence.

EXAMPLE: Angela and Maria decided to try online dating.
~~Angela and Maria~~ are long-time best friends.

SOLUTION: Angela and Maria, long-time best friends, decided to try online dating.

1. They found the ideal site to begin their search.
   The site matched single medical professionals.

2. Angela wanted to connect with other singles right away.
   Angela was an enthusiastic online dater.

3. But Maria wanted to take her time and review the site thoroughly.
   Maria is an introvert.

4. Maria needed to meet someone who could deal with her busy schedule.
   Maria was an emergency-room nurse.

5. But Angela liked to date people who wouldn't mind her hectic schedule.
   Angela was a doctor with long and erratic hours.

6. Angela also differed with Maria when it came to age.
   Angela was interested in older men.

7. But besides an interest in online dating, Angela and Maria had at least two things in common.
   The two things in common were an interest finding true love and a desire to get married.

8. They made a plan in case one of them found her soul mate.
   The plan included introducing the man to the other, spending time as a group, and being respectful of each other's privacy.

Exercise Two Not So Typical Music Listeners

Combine each group of sentences below by reducing the last two sentences in each group to appositives that modify nouns in the first sentence. Note that the nouns aren't underlined, so look to see what is being repeated and cross out repeated nouns and forms of the verb *be* before you do any sentence combining.

EXAMPLE: Most people enjoy music.
~~The people are~~ males and females of any age.
~~Music is~~ a kind of medicine for the soul.

SOLUTION: Most people, males and females of any age, enjoy music, a kind of medicine for the soul.

1. Heavy metal is supposed to attract crowds of long-haired, maladjusted teens.
Heavy metal is music with loud electric guitars and drums.
The maladjusted teens are young people who rebel against their parents.

2. But my Uncle Walter enjoys listening to heavy metal.
Uncle Walter is a 40-year-old, bald accountant.
His heavy metal is usually some song by Black Sabbath.

3. On the other hand, reggae is supposed to attract hordes of modern teenagers.
Reggae is music developed in Jamaica.
The teenagers are teens who dream of dating the lead singers.

4. But my Aunt Wilma listens to reggae.
Aunt Wilma is a 50-year-old housewife.
Reggae is any song by Bob Marley.

5. Soft rock is supposed to attract people like Walter and Wilma.
   Soft rock is background music often played in elevators.
   Walter and Wilma are people who wear polyester suits.

6. Yet Walter and Wilma's 13-year-old daughter loves listening to soft rock.
   Their daughter is Winnifred.
   Soft rock is any Barry Manilow song that plays in elevators or dentists' offices.

7. Rap music songs are supposed to attract only young people.
   The songs are usually popular ballads that need no instruments.
   The young people are those who want a message with a beat.

8. However, Walter's mother really gets into rap.
   Walter's mother is a 75-year-old woman with arthritis.
   Rap is her excuse to limber up her joints.

Creating Appositives

Writers can use noun phrase appositives effectively to give readers helpful, specific information and to condense their many ideas in a logical and sophisticated way. In the previous exercises, you practiced combining sentences; in the following exercise, you will create some of your own appositives. The nouns to be modified are underlined, and blanks are provided so that you can add specific information with appositives.

EXAMPLE: Too many people today need to find a suitable companion,

____

SOLUTION: Too many people today need to find a suitable companion, a dog who loves them unconditionally, a cat who keeps them warm at night, a guinea pig who never complains about the cooking, or a spouse with a large bank account.

Exercise Three Alfred and Edward

1. My friend Alfred spends his afternoons watching his favorite program on "Trash T.V.,"

____

2. On the other hand, my cousin Edward spends his afternoons at his favorite video stores in the mall—

____

____

3. Finally bored with their usual pastimes, Alfred and Edward met me last Friday at my favorite club,

____

4. Alfred and Edward, two ____________________, danced the night away with some lovely women, and they learned some of the following songs:

____

____

5. But the next day, Alfred went back to his old habit, ____________________, and Edward went back to the local mall, ____________________.

____

Exercise Four Madge and Mordred

What follows is a hypothetical love story, one that features the meeting and eventual marriage of Madge and Mordred. You are to fill in the blanks with noun phrase modifiers (appositives). If you have any difficulty coming up with appositives, try asking yourself some questions about the underlined nouns.

Madge, (1) ______________________________, was a newly divorced woman. So she decided to try a computer dating service and called her friend Mary Frances, (2) ______________________________, someone who had signed up with many agencies in the past. Mary Frances told Madge to contact the Best Bet Dating Spa, (3) ______________________________. Mary Frances promised Madge that she was sure to meet with success. On Saturday morning, Madge left her apartment, (4) ______________________________, and set out for the Best Bet Spa. The spa, on the corner of Fifth Street and Vine, looked like an impressive structure, (5) ______________________________. Inside, Madge met the director, Mr. Rogers, (6) ______________________________, someone she felt very comfortable talking to. After she filled out the application, she went home and waited. Later that week, Madge's phone, (7) ______________________________, rang. A young man named Mordred was on the line and said, in a voice that grabbed Madge immediately, that he had gotten her number from Best Bet. Mordred said he knew they were meant for each other when he heard that they like the same kinds of music—(8) ______________________________. Mordred also suggested that they go on a date the next week, and Madge readily accepted, agreeing to meet him on Friday night at Woof, Purr, Whistle and Thump, his favorite hangout, (9) ______________________________. When they met, Madge first noticed Mordred's eyes, (10) ______________________________, and Mordred fell in love with Madge's feet, (11) ______________________________. Actually, it was love at first sight for both. Married now for three years, Madge and Mordred share their dreams, (12) ______________________________.

Exercise Five You Be the Author

1. Write a sentence in which you use an appositive to describe a movie or a singing group you enjoy.

2. Write a sentence in which you use an appositive to describe a car you'd like to have.

3. Write a sentence in which you use an appositive to describe your best friend.

4. Write a sentence in which you use an appositive to describe your favorite form of entertainment.

5. Write a sentence in which you use an appositive to describe your favorite place.

Next, write five sentences about the topic you're currently writing about in your writing class, and try to use appositives to describe some of the nouns in your sentences.

6.

7.

8.

9.

10.

Sense of Time

Review Exercise 7

Join the sentences below by adding noun modifiers (adjectives, prepositional phrases, and appositives) to the base sentences and by joining sentences using coordinators, subordinators, and parallel structures. The nouns to be modified are underlined, and joining techniques are given in brackets. Cross out any repeated words and forms of *be* in the sentences containing modifiers.

EXAMPLE: Most of us think about our future.
~~The future is~~ the next hour.
~~The future is~~ the next day.
~~The future is~~ the next week.
[coordinator—contrast] The future may be years from now.

SOLUTION: Most of us think about our future—the next hour, the next day, or the next week—but the future may be years from now.

1. ***[subordinator—time]*** We think about the future.
We are forced to make decisions.
The decisions are about our education, career, and family.
The decisions are based on our motivation.
The decisions are based on our attitude toward risk-taking.
The decisions are based on our sense of obligation.

2. Some people need to make plans for the rest of their lives.
These people are future-oriented.
These people are the ones who make daily lists of their goals.
[subordinator—contrast] Other people live each day as if it were their last.
These people are present-oriented.
These people are the ones who live for the moment.

3. All research studies agree that our "time sense" can greatly affect our lives.
[coordinator—contrast] Some studies have shown that attitudes toward the future differ according to age, sex, income, and occupation.

4. According to a study done by Alexander Gonzales, most adults are more concerned about the future than teenagers are.
The adults are those 40 years old or older.
[coordinator—effect] This future planning is a tendency that increases with age.

5. In addition, the study claims that middle-aged men are more likely to plan for the future than middle-aged women are.
The men are generally fathers and professionals responsible for their families' financial security.
The women are usually housewives and mothers who have achieved their goals.
[coordinator—contrast] Perhaps these attitudes will change as women and men change their expectations.
The expectations are of their roles in society.

6. People who earn poor salaries worry mainly about the present.
The salaries are incomes less than $16,000 per year.
[coordinator—contrast] They may tend to be fatalistic individuals.
The individuals are people who believe that for them, no future exists.

7. People tend to fall into both camps.
The people are with higher incomes.
The camps are those who live for the moment.
The camps are those who make goals and subgoals.
[coordinator—cause] These people can afford to make choices.

8. Finally, according to the study, most people tend to pick certain occupations for themselves.
[subordinator—cause] They may already have the time sense needed for the chosen occupation.

Unit Thirteen

Modifying Nouns with Adjective Clauses

In this unit, you will again be working with structures that modify nouns—adjective clauses. Like appositives, adjective clauses are a good way to add descriptive details to nouns. The following sentences contain adjective clauses:

> The student who aced his exam was happy.
> The exam, which covered six chapters of trigonometry, determined the final course grade.

We call the underlined structures "adjective clauses" because, like simple adjectives, they describe nouns. In the above sentences, the adjective clause *who aced his exam* describes the noun *student*, and the adjective clause *which covered six chapters of trigonometry* describes the noun *exam*.

We call the underlined structures "clauses" because they are made up of a subject—*who*, *that*, or *which*—and a verb. But they are dependent clauses, so they cannot be sentences by themselves. And like other modifiers of more than one word, they come after the nouns they modify.

In the exercises in this unit, you will be joining two sentences by making the second one into an adjective clause. Follow these steps:

1. Find the word in the second sentence that either repeats or refers to the underlined noun in the first sentence.
2. Cross out the word that you found and change it to *who*, *that*, or *which*.
3. Change the second sentence into an adjective clause and place it in the first sentence after the noun it modifies.

The following are examples and explanations for the combined sentences using adjective clauses.

Example A: Mary is a volunteer English teacher in the Marshall Islands.
who ~~Mary~~ grew up in California.

Solution: Mary, who grew up in California, is a volunteer English teacher in the Marshall Islands.

Explanation: *Mary* is repeated in the second sentence and is a person word, so *Mary* can be replaced with *who*.

Example B: The students study their core subjects in English.
who ~~They~~ usually spend most of their lives on the islands.

SOLUTION: The students, who spend most of their lives on the islands, study their core subjects in English.

EXPLANATION: *They* in the second sentence refers back to *students* in the first sentence. Here *they* refers to people, so *they* can be replaced with *who*.

EXAMPLE C: Many volunteers live with island families in thatched-roof huts.
that ~~The huts~~ don't have electricity or running water.

SOLUTION: Many volunteers live with island families in thatched-roof huts that don't have electricity or running water.

EXPLANATION: *Huts* is repeated in the second sentence, and *huts* are things, so *huts* can be replaced with *that*.

EXAMPLE D: The Marshall Islands are located in the central Pacific Ocean.
which ~~They~~ consist of five islands and 29 atolls.

SOLUTION: The Marshall Islands, which consist of five islands and 29 atolls, are located in the central Pacific Ocean.

EXPLANATION: *They* in the second sentence refers back to *Marshall Islands* in the first sentence, and *islands* are things, so *they* can be replaced by *which*.

EXAMPLE E: The land area is only 70 square miles.
Coconut trees dominate ~~it~~. Which

SOLUTION: The land area, which coconut trees dominate, is only 70 square miles.

EXPLANATION: *It* in the second sentence refers to *area* in the first sentence. Since *it* is a thing, we can replace *it* with *which*. We change the word order in the adjective clause so that *which* follows the noun it modifies.

EXAMPLE F: The Marshallese value children.
whose ~~Their~~ families are usually large.

SOLUTION: The Marshallese, whose families are usually large, value children.

EXPLANATION: *Their* in the second sentence refers to *the Marshallese* in the first sentence. *There* is a possessive word that refers to people or things, so we can replace *their* with *whose*.

Exercise One Rock Climbing

In each of the sentence pairs below, a noun or pronoun in the second sentence either repeats or refers to a noun in the first sentence. Change the noun in the second sentence to *who*, *which*, or *that* so that the second sentence can become an adjective clause modifying a noun in the first sentence.

EXAMPLE: My good friend Andrew likes to participate in rock climbing.
He claims to like adventure.

SOLUTION: My good friend Andrew, who claims to like adventure, likes to participate in rock climbing.

1. The rock climbing requires Andrew to take precautions.
   It involves him wearing kneepads.

2. Often, Andrew goes with a friend.
   He acts as a spotter.

3. To fully prepare, Andrew must thoroughly plan his climb.
   It covers the entire mountain.

4. He must also follow his plan carefully to get to the top.
   He will reach it without injury with good planning.

5. To be fully protected and safe, Andrew wears special shoes and pants.
   They are appropriate rock-climbing clothing.

6. He also wears a climbing helmet.
   It is made of hard plastic.

7. As Andrew does his climb, he listens to the sounds of nature.
   They help calm him during the ascent.

8. During his excursion, Andrew raises his heart rate.
   He needs no other stimulant.

9. Yet through it all, he experiences a calm feeling.
   His climbing friends experience it too.

Exercise Two The Lonesome Cowboy

In the last exercise with sentence pairs, you reduced some sentences to adjective clauses by looking for repeated nouns or pronoun referents such as *she* or *it* that could be replaced with *who*, *which*, or *that*. Then you modified nouns with your new adjective clauses. The following exercise is similar, but it introduces another common signal for reducing some sentences to adjective clauses. Look at the examples and the solutions to reducing some sentences to adjective clauses, making for a smoother sentence overall.

EXAMPLE: Many people romanticize American cowboys.
These cowboys rode the cattle trails after the Civil War.

SOLUTION: Many people romanticize American cowboys <u>who rode the cattle trails after the Civil War</u>.

EXPLANATION: We have turned the second sentence into an adjective clause, modifying *cowboys* in the first sentence. The signal here is the word *these*, which is a repeated noun. Also watch for the signals *this, that*, and *those*.

1. Cowboys actually were overworked and underpaid.
These cowboys rode endless miles in rough weather.

2. Cowboys rarely got enough sleep.
Those cowboys worked 18 hours a day, every day of the week.

3. Cowboys ate a boring daily diet.
This diet usually consisted of beans, bacon, cornbread, and coffee.

4. Cowboys often sang songs around campfires.
Those songs revealed their loneliness and hard lives.

5. But cowboys rarely complained.
   Those cowboys had a lot to complain about.

6. Each cowboy found a way to entertain himself.
   This cowboy couldn't have a normal family life.

7. Some cowboys bought magazines.
   Cowboys read and passed along these magazines.

8. A cowboy's prized possession was his hat.
   He wore that hat during meals and sometimes to bed.

9. Cowboys also valued their boots.
   These boots often cost two months' wages.

10. People still commonly believe that cowboys were heroes.
    These heroes stand for the freedom of the Wild West.

Special Rule: Who/Whom

So far, you have used adjective clauses that begin with *who, that*, or *which*. Although you may need to refer to the previous section for some of the following exercises, this section will primarily clarify the difference between *who* and *whom*. Although both *who* and *whom* begin adjective clauses that modify person nouns, each has a separate grammatical function in the adjective clause it begins.

Take, for example, the following sentences containing adjective clauses:

My brother, [*who* married a crazy woman], has one crazy baby.
My sister-in-law, [*whom* my mother dislikes], is a fanatic.

Why do we use *who* in one adjective clause and *whom* in the other?

If we take the adjective clauses and turn them into sentences by replacing *who* or *whom* with a personal pronoun, we have the answer:

ADJECTIVE CLAUSE:

(my brother)	(my sister-in-law)
who married a crazy woman	whom my mother dislikes

SENTENCE:

He married a crazy woman.	My mother dislikes her.

EXPLANATION: The pronoun you placed in your sentence signals you to use

WHO for subject pronouns:	**WHOM for object pronouns:**
HE	HIM
SHE	HER
WE	US
THEY	THEM

REVIEW: To decide whether to use *who* or *whom*, follow these steps:

1. Identify and underline the words that make up the adjective clause.
2. Turn the adjective clause into a sentence by replacing *who* or *whom* with a personal pronoun from the previous list.
3. If you use a subject pronoun, use *who*, but if you use an object pronoun, use *whom*.

EXAMPLE:
1. Our postman, who/whom is usually prompt, arrived late.
2. He is usually prompt.
3. He = *who*.

Exercise Three Cat Adopts Man

Follow the steps in the previous example and decide whether *who* or *whom is correct for the given sentence.* In the first four sentences, Step 2 is done for you and gives you some additional information which should help you decide between *who* or *whom*.

1. Joey, (*who/whom*) lived alone, decided to get a new roommate.
   (He lived alone.)

2. Joey's new roommate, Millie, (*who/whom*) Joey found in the local animal shelter, turned out to be a cat.
   (Joey found her in the local animal shelter.)

3. When they first met at the shelter, Millie, (*who/whom*) knew that Joey was the one for her, jumped onto Joey's lap and started purring.
   (She knew that Joey was the one for her.)

4. Joey, (*who/whom*) immediately adored Millie, decided to adopt her and take her home.
   (He immediately adored Millie.)

5. But Joey, (*who/whom*) Millie recognized as the perfect roommate the moment she saw him, was actually chosen by Millie.

6. After they got home, Millie, (*who/whom*) Joey promptly gave cat treats, began to settle in.

7. Joey, (*who/whom*) hoped that Millie would keep mice away, discovered that Millie liked to bring mice home.

8. Millie brought gifts of mice to Joey, (*who/whom*) she wanted to please.

9. Now Joey has the perfect roommate (*who/whom*) delights him in every way except one.

10. Millie, (*who/whom*) everyone recognizes as an affectionate, smart, and endearing companion for Joey, shows no signs of giving up hunting mice.

Exercise Four Stranger Than Fiction

In this exercise, you will be given two or three sentences. Note what noun or pronoun in the second sentence either repeats or refers to a noun in the first sentence. Then turn the second sentence into an adjective clause beginning with *who, whom, that, which,* or *whose*, and modify the noun in the first sentence with your new adjective clause. (In exercise 4 and exercise 7, you will create two adjective clauses.)

EXAMPLE: Reba collects newspaper clippings.
The clippings contain bizarre true stories about people.

SOLUTION: Reba collects newspaper clippings that contain bizarre true stories about people.

1. In one story, a man was fishing when his boat capsized.
The man was only 18 years old.

2. After drifting on his overturned boat, the man decided to try to swim to land and was rescued by a stingray.
The stingray put him on his back and carried him to safety over 450 miles in 13 days.

3. In another story, a man was given a public bath by fellow villagers in Kenya.
The man had not bathed in three years.

4. The villagers then gave the man new clean clothes and took him to the barber for a free haircut and a shave.
The new clean clothes replaced the old dirty ones.
The old dirty ones were burned by the villagers.

5. The day of cleansing ended with a trip to a bar for several beers.
   The man's new friends paid for the beers.

6. Perhaps the weirdest story is about eight elderly Belgian nuns.
   The nuns sold their convent.

7. With their profits, the nuns bought a limousine and racehorses.
   They paid for the limousine by check.
   They left the racehorses in Belgium.

8. But Reba's favorite story is about a man and his homemade flying machine.
   His flying machine consisted of a lawn chair attached to 45 helium weather balloons and loaded with snacks, beer, a radio, and a pellet gun.

9. The lawn chair finally descended after he methodically shot the balloons with his pellet gun.
   The lawn chair rose to about 15,000 feet and flew near the Los Angeles airport.

10. The lawn chair pilot landed on the ground and was greeted by the Long Beach Police.
    The pilot never intended to fly more than 30 feet above his own backyard.

Exercise Five Rio

Like appositives, adjective clauses enable writers to effectively join their ideas and show their readers what they mean. So it makes sense not only to practice joining ideas using adjective clauses, but also to create adjective clause modifiers.

Given here is a hypothetical mystery story in which there are nouns that could be made more specific with adjective clauses, although you might also want to use a few appositives. The nouns to be modified are underlined, and blanks for your modifiers are provided.

One day, Matilda sat in a cafe, sipping cappuccino and talking with her friend Zsa-Zsa,

(1)____. Matilda was telling

Zsa-Zsa about her husband merve, (2) ______________________________

Apparently, Merv had turned into a very mysterious man, (3) __________________

__________ , and Matilda suspected that he was now involved in some criminal activity

(4) ____________________. Recently, Merv brought home some very disgusting

friends (5) ____________________________________. And he purchased

three expensive new cars, (6) ______________________________.

But when Matilda, (7) ____

questioned Merv about his activities, he ran out the front door. Despondent,

Matilda knew that her best friend Zsa-Zsa would know how to solve the problem,

(8) _____________________________________. Zsa-Zsa recommended

that Matilda do one of two things: hire a private detective to find out what Merv had got-

ten himself into or sell the cars and run away to Rio. Matilda decided to hire a detective

(9) ____________________________________. So the next day, the

detective she'd hired followed Merv to work and to his favorite hangout,

(10) ____. But

unfortunately, the detective lost Merv when Merv entered a K-Mart. When the detective

tried to call Matilda to let her know what had happened, a policewoman,

(11) ____________________________________ answered the phone.

The policewoman informed the detective that Matilda (12) ________________

__________________, had been arrested at the airport for possession of a stolen car,

(13) __________________________________, and that Zsa-Zsa was last seen

boarding a plane, holding a cup of cappuccino in one hand and an airline ticket to Rio in

the other.

Exercise Six You Be the Author

1. Write a sentence in which you use an adjective clause to describe a person you know.

2. Write a sentence in which you use an adjective clause to describe your home.

3. Write a sentence in which you use an adjective clause to describe a home you'd like to own.

4. Write a sentence in which you use an adjective clause to describe a book you've read. (The noun you describe can be the title of the book.)

5. Write a sentence in which you use an adjective clause to describe a place you often visit.

Next, write five sentences about the topic you're currently writing about in your writing class. Try to use adjective clauses to describe the people, things, or ideas you're writing about.

6.

7.

8.

9.

10.

Unit Fourteen

Modifying Sentences with Verbal Phrases

Verbals are verb parts that modify the subject of a sentence. In other words, they are not the actions associated with the verb; they function as nouns, adjectives, or adverbs. Although verbs in sentences tell the time, or tense, verbals do not; they have other functions in sentences.

Let's take a look at what that means. Three verbal forms—the *-ing* form as in when honk becomes *honking*, or present participle; the *-ed* form as in when *honk* becomes *honked*, or past participle; and the *to* form, or infinitive as in *to honk*—can be used to form verbal phrases. (See Unit One for a review of present and past participle verb forms.)

The following examples show different verb forms in sentences. Here, you can see how the verbal phrases come from verbs and how verbals can be used to make your sentences more concise and clear:

EXAMPLE 1: Jamari was hoping to attract Jeff's attention.
Jamari honked her horn loudly.

SOLUTION: Hoping to attract Jeff's attention, Jamari honked her horn loudly.
OR: Jamari honked her horn loudly, hoping to attract Jeff's attention.

EXAMPLE 2: Jeff was frightened by the frantic honking.
He got off the freeway at the first exit.

SOLUTION: Frightened by the frantic honking, Jeff got off the freeway at the first exit.
OR: Jeff got off the freeway at the first exit, frightened by the frantic honking.

EXAMPLE 3: Jamari wanted to find Jeff.
She got off at the next exit and doubled back.

SOLUTION: To find Jeff, Jamari got off at the next exit and doubled back.
OR: Jamari got off at the next exit and doubled back to find Jeff.

Verbal phrases are good ways to show that two actions happened at the same time:

1. *hoping/honked*
2. *frightened /got off*
3. *to find/got off*

But often verbal phrases also show the purpose of an action in the sentence:

1. *Jamari honked her horn. Why? Because she was hoping to attract Jeff's attention.*
2. *Jeff got off the freeway. Why? Because he was frightened by the frantic honking.*
3. *Jamari got off at the next exit. Why? Because she wanted to find Jeff.*

So verbal phrases have two functions:

1. To show a time relationship between the action in the verbal phrase and the action in the main clause of the sentence.
2. To show the purpose of the action in the main clause.

When you use verbal phrases, you have to follow one important rule: The doer of the action in the verbal phrase is usually the sentence subject. As a general rule, that doer has to be a noun or pronoun in the main clause of the sentence.

In sentence 1, who was hoping to attract Jeff's attention? ________________

Who honked her horn? ________________

Notice that the following sentence does not make sense:

Incorrect: Reaching out her right arm, the ball was dunked into the basket.

The verbal phrase does not make sense with the subject of the sentence because the noun *ball* cannot do the action *reaching*. To correct this sentence, make the sentence subject be a noun that can do the action in the verbal phrase:

Correct: Reaching out her right arm, the player dunked the ball into the basket.

Exercise One Going Out to Eat

Join the sets of sentences in the exercise, making the second sentence into a verbal phrase. You may place the verbal phrase before or after the main sentence; you will have to decide whether or not the verbal phrase can make sense in either position. (Sometimes the verbal phrase will only make sense in one of these positions.)

EXAMPLE: Rita read the latest restaurant reviews.
She wanted to find a good restaurant.

SOLUTION: To find a good restaurant, Rita read the latest restaurant reviews.
OR Rita read the latest restaurant reviews to find a good restaurant.

1. Jamal and Rita studied the "Yellow Pages" all Saturday afternoon.
They were looking for a good restaurant that would please Rita's parents.

2. Jamal offered to help pay for the dinner.
He was hoping Rita would go for a steakhouse.

3. Rita refused his offer.
She was accustomed to paying her own way.

4. She also vetoed the steakhouse idea.
She was concerned that her vegetarian mother would feel left out at a steak house.

5. Jamal suggested a vegetarian diner called "The Lean Bean."
He wanted to simplify the problem.

6. But Rita rejected this suggestion also.
   She was exclaiming that "The Lean Bean" served tasteless alfalfa hot dogs and rubbery soybean "chicken."

7. She said they should find a restaurant that also served meat.
   She was thinking of her carnivorous dad.

8. Jamal and Rita began to bicker.
   They were frustrated at their failure to find a satisfactory restaurant.

9. Jamal finally noticed the name, in tiny print, of a Middle Eastern restaurant.
   He was desperately seeking a place that would please everyone.

10. Rita phoned "Ali's Place" for their list of dinner entrees.
    She wanted to be on the safe side.

11. The restaurant served juicy skewered lamb for Rita's father and spicy meatless falafel for her mother.
    It was offering a diverse assortment of entrees.

12. Jamal and Rita left the restaurant smiling that night.
    They were satisfied with their selection.

Exercise Two The Iron Horse

Just as you did in Exercise One, join the sets of sentences below.

EXAMPLE: In the United States, railroads were first used in the late 18th century. They were used to haul coal from mines or transport people short distances around a few cities.

SOLUTION: In the United States, railroads were first used in the late 18th century to haul coal from mines or transport people short distances around a few cities.

EXPLANATION: The second sentence tells the reason for the action in the first sentence—*to haul coal from mines or transport people short distances around a few cities.* Since the *to* (or infinitive) verbal shows the reason or purpose for an action, the *to* verbal is a logical choice.

1. The railroad cars were pulled by horses.
   The railroad cars were very slow.

2. But in the late 18th century, the steam engine was invented.
   The steam engine was providing a way to pull railroad cars faster and farther than horses.

3. The steam trains were known as "iron horses."
   The steam trains raced horse-drawn trains, but the steam trains always won.

4. By the 1930s and 1940s, steam engines were huge,
   The steam engines were pulling 100-car freight trains and 100 mph passenger trains.

5. The train tracks were pounded by the huge driving wheels on the steam trains.
   The tracks frequently had to be replaced.

Exercise Three The Vegetable Garden

Verbal phrases can often be good alternatives to subordinate clauses—also called *dependent clauses*—that show cause/effect or time relationships. (Remember, a subordinate or dependent clause cannot stand on its own as a grammatical part of a sentence.) In this exercise, you'll revise the sentences by making the underlined subordinate clauses into verbal phrases. Notice that the subject of each subordinate clause beginning with *because* and *since* or *before*, *after* and *while* is also the subject of the main clause; that's your clue that you can make the subordinate clause into a verbal phrase.

EXAMPLE: Because she wanted to eat better,
Mary planted a vegetable garden.

SOLUTION: **(In order) to eat better,**
Mary planted a vegetable garden.

EXAMPLE: After she planted her seeds,
Mary watered the site.

SOLUTION: **After planting the seeds,** Mary watered the site.

1. Because she wanted variety in her garden,
Mary researched different vegetables.

2. Since he hoped to learn gardening,
Nathan helped Mary plant tomatoes.

3. Before planting the garden,
Mary tilled the soil.

4. Because she knew the soil was hard,
Mary dug with a sharp shovel.

5. Before he planted the tomatoes,
Nathan donned gloves.

6. While she was planting,
Mary took frequent breaks.

7. After he finished planting the tomatoes,
Nathan made a wish that they would grow.

8. Because she knew the basics of gardening,
Mary felt confident that her vegetables would grow quickly.

9. After she saw how much he had planted,
Mary told Nathan to take a break.

10. Since they wanted to celebrate,
They drank a toast to their garden.

Creating Verbal Phrases

Exercise Four Fitness Folly

Create your own *-ing*, *-ed*, and *to* verbal phrases to complete the sentences in the exercise. Remember that a noun in the main clause must be able to do the action in the verbal phrase. Most likely, you will have an easier time coming up with *-ing* phrases, but try to come up with the two other forms as well.

EXAMPLE: ________________, Ethel decided she should get in shape.

SOLUTION: Looking in the mirror, Ethel decided she should get in shape.

1. ________________________________, Ethel wanted to find an exercise plan she could stick to.
2. She tried aerobics, ________________________________.
3. But poor Ethel, ________________________________, embarrassed herself in front of the whole class.
4. ________________________________, she gave up on aerobics and turned to ballet.
5. ________________________________, she had to give up on ballet, too.
6. ________________________________, Ethel began lessons at the local swimming pool, ________________________________.
7. ________________________________, Ethel discovered she was allergic to chlorine!
8. Ethel, ________________________________, decided to take up a martial art.
9. She was a success at this activity, so she's been practicing it ever since, ________________________________.
10. ________________________________ makes Ethel feel strong and vibrant.